Michael Tomkinson's

GAMBIA

First published 1987 by
Michael Tomkinson Publishing
Hammamet Tunisia &
POB 215 Oxford OX2 0NR
Reprinted 1991
Second edition 2000

Designed by
Roger Davies Gregory Taylor

Photograph page 108 by Tony
Baker/Picturepoint; pages 28 left, 29 upper
left, 33, 34, 35 right, 36, 71 lower, 76 left, 104 by
Eddie Brewer OBE; pages 81, 92 inset by Ann
Hills; pages 71 upper, 118 by Michael Kirtley;
pages 1, 3 upper left & lower right, 7 upper left
& lower right, 18 centre & upper, 20, 21 right,
22, 22-23, 31 right, 46 upper, 48 upper right
and lower, 50, 51, 52 upper & left, 53 upper, 55,
62 left, 69 lower, 73 upper, 75 upper, 76 right,
80 upper, 81 inset, 90-91, 90 left & centre, 91,
96, 119 lower, 126-27 lower, facing page 128 by
Michel Renaudeau/Hoa-Qui; pages 1, 3 upper
right & lower left, 4-5, 4 upper left, 5 right, 6
upper right, 7 centre left, 14-15, 18 lower right,
19, 21 left, 25 inset, 26 inset, 28 centre, 28-29,
32, 44-45, 46 left, 52 lower, 54 left, 58-59, 62-
63, 84 lower right, 98-99, 100-101, 103 upper,
106 upper, 110 lower, 115, 116-17 by The
Gambia Experience; pages 7 upper right &
centre, 45 centre, 59 right, 72 lower, 82 lower,
84 lower left, 85 lower by Thomson Holidays;
pages 38, 39 by James Walford; all others by
the author

Printed in Singapore by
Star Standard Industries
ISBN 0 905500 59 8 (hardback)
ISBN 0 905500 64 4 (paperback)

Contents

Introduction

In a world where racial discrimination, ethnic violence, sectarian strife and civil war are all too frequent, finding a country free of all these is refreshing. It is perhaps a sign of the times that such havens of peace go unnoticed. That in The Gambia more ethnic groups than Bosnia's cohabit uneventfully does not interest the media. The press is not impressed by the fact that Gambian Muslims, Christians and animists – a divergence of faiths far wider than Ulster's – live and work together unconcerned by each other's beliefs. That religious, racial and sexual abuses are unknown here is not news.

More and more visitors are discovering individually what the mass media ignore. Despite continuing economic decline and a recent peacable change of regime, this smallest nation in Africa is attracting an ever greater number of holidaymakers from Europe.

Their destination is the closest of the English-speaking Commonwealth countries, Britain's first and last West African colony and the tropical resort within easiest reach of Europe in which winter sun and warmth are guaranteed. The Gambia's island-capital borders the estuary of the magnificent watercourse from which the modern state takes its name, shape and *raison d'être*. Early adventurers sailed up this 'Golden

River' in search of legendary mines. Later traders came, lured by gold and ivory, but soon turning their attention more to lading slaves. For Mungo Park and his lesser-known contemporaries the river was the long-sought route to the riches of Timbuktu, to the source of the Niger and even the Nile. While 19th-century officials on the spot palavered and pacified, their governments, scrambling for Africa, haggled and aggrandized, encompassing the Gambia in artificial frontiers. The legacy today is Senegambian families in which, beside their local languages, some speak English, some French. And a relaxed and peaceful river that, by pleasure boat, dug-out or converted pirogue, you can travel in relative comfort

two arterial roads criss-cross the country. There are roughly a dozen accessible ancient sites, a half-dozen interesting churches and mosques, three national parks (one out of bounds), three nature reserves and only three town-ships with fridges and cold drinks in The Gambia's whole northern half.

But neither should the attractions be under-estimated. The broad sandy beaches,

sufferance, a post-colonial anachronism. It has a character and identity of its own. Here people have moved and married so freely, so blithely ignoring what authorities call porous borders, that the country's smallness is compensated by its 'quintessential' richness, by the insight it offers into the region around. You can holiday in Kenya and learn nothing of its neighbours, visit Tunisia without suffering the side-effects

viewing villages and wildlife little changed by the 20th century.

In sunshine rarely interrupted between October and May, in a welcome winter average of 24°C, modern beach hotels stand for the most part in gardens ablaze with flowers: hibiscus, frangipani, bougainvillea and Morning glory, Golden shower, lantana, jacaranda and canna lilies come as a dazzling contrast to British winter-grey. The Gambians' everyday dress is equally colourful and, usually just as brightly flamboyant, birds abound everywhere, in a profusion that has made the country famous.

Outside the hotels, standards should not be overstated: the capital, Banjul, is the largest town – with 45,000 inhabitants. Just

strewn with shells, are everywhere uncrowded. Cottonsilk and baobab trees tower over villages where fishermen and farmers gather at the *bantaba*; women pound coos or pump water, their babies on their backs, while dewlapped cattle graze by mountains of groundnuts and high-piled kapok or cotton. Baboons patrol and palm-trees dominate the half-farmed savanna around, which gives way to lush 'jungle' beside the streams and hollows. And through all this runs one of Africa's great waterways, tapering eastward for some 300 miles.

Even more than the bird life and flora, I find the population fascinating. Though small and endowed with few natural resources, The Gambia is by no means a state on

of Libya or Algeria, but The Gambia means an encounter with all the colourfulness, friendliness and penury of West Africa.

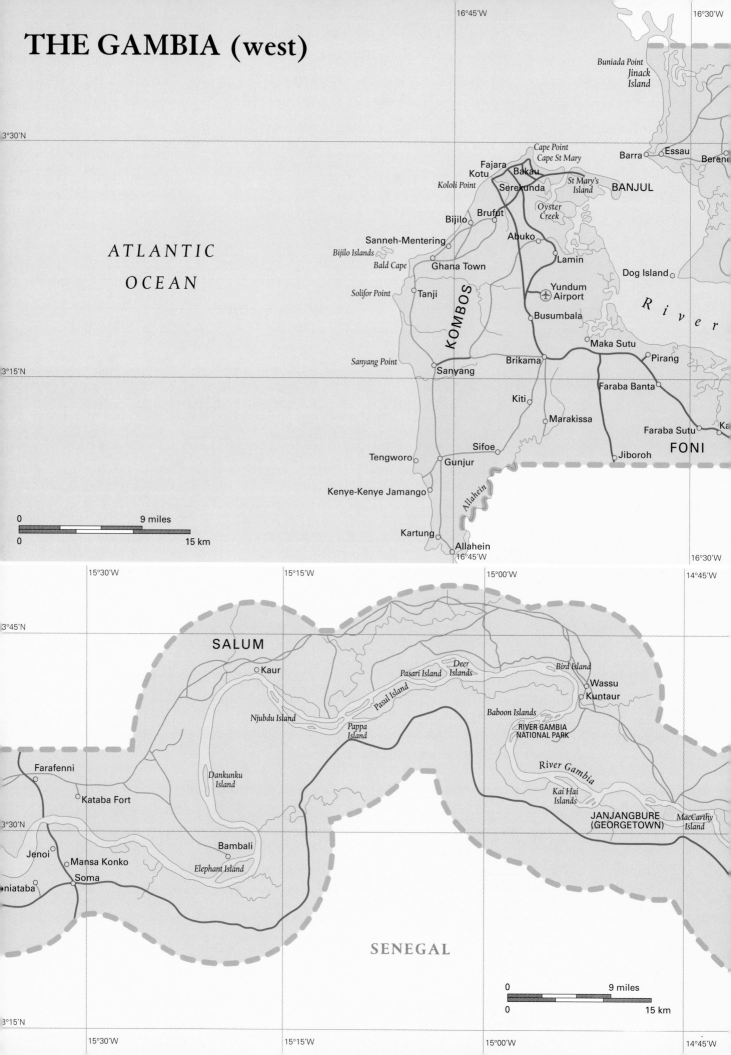

THE GAMBIA (west)

ATLANTIC OCEAN

16°45'W · 16°30'W

3°30'N

Buniada Point
Jinack Island

Barra · Essau · Bere

Cape Point
Cape St Mary

Fajara
Kotu · Bakau
Kololi Point · Serekunda · *St Mary's Island* · **BANJUL**

Bijilo · Brufut · *Oyster Creek*

Sanneh-Mentering · Abuko

Bijilo Islands · Lamin

Bald Cape · Ghana Town · Dog Island

Solifor Point · Tanji · **KOMBOS** · Yundum Airport · *River*

Busumbala

Sanyang Point · Maka Sutu

Brikama · Pirang

Sanyang · Faraba Banta

Kiti · Faraba Sutu · Ka

Marakissa · **FONI**

Tengworo · Sifoe · Gunjur · Jiboroh

Kenye-Kenye Jamango

Allahein

Kartung · Allahein
16°45'W · 16°30'W

| 0 | | 9 miles |
| 0 | | 15 km |

15°30'W · 15°15'W · 15°00'W · 14°45'W

3°45'N

SALUM

Kaur

Pasari Island · *Deer Islands* · *Bird Island*

Pasul Island · Wassu · Kuntaur

Njubdu Island

Baboon Islands

Pappa Island · **RIVER GAMBIA NATIONAL PARK**

Farafenni · *Dankunku Island* · *River Gambia*

Kataba Fort · *Kai Hai Islands*

3°30'N · **JANJANGBURE (GEORGETOWN)** · *MacCarthy Island*

Bambali

Jenoi · Mansa Konko

niataba · Soma · *Elephant Island*

SENEGAL

3°15'N

15°30'W · 15°15'W · 15°00'W · 14°45'W

| 0 | | 9 miles |
| 0 | | 15 km |

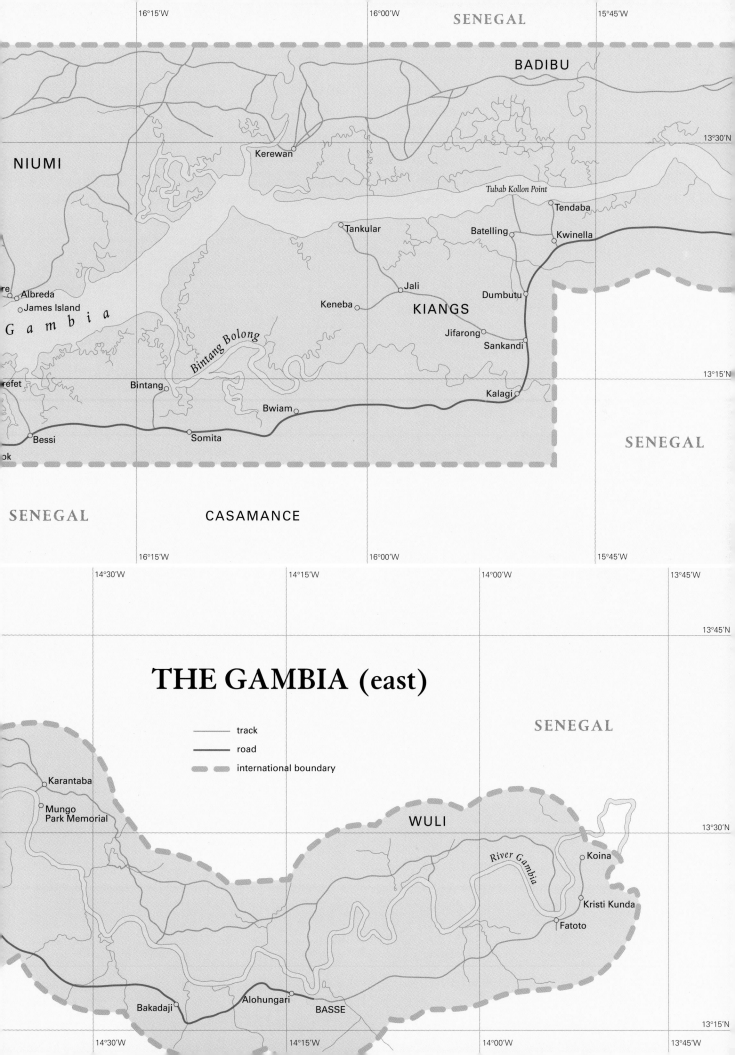

SENEGAL

BADIBU

NIUMI

Kerewan

Tubab Kollon Point

Tendaba

Tankular

Batelling

Kwinella

Albreda

James Island

Jali

Dumbutu

Gambia

Keneba

KIANGS

Jifarong

Bintang Bolong

Sankandi

Bintang

Kalagi

refet

Bwiam

SENEGAL

Bessi

Somita

ok

SENEGAL

CASAMANCE

THE GAMBIA (east)

	track
	road
	international boundary

SENEGAL

Karantaba

WULI

Mungo
Park Memorial

River Gambia

Koina

Kristi Kunda

Fatoto

Bakadaji

Alohungari

BASSE

Geography

The Gambia is the westernmost country of Africa (which is why Lufthansa chose it in 1934 as base for the first-ever transatlantic flights) and lies astride longitude 15°W (which is why today's six-hour flight from Britain causes very little jet-lag). It is equidistant from the Equator and the Tropic of Cancer, 13°15'-13°30'N being the approximate latitudinal extent. In common with many of its African neighbours, the country is the victim of some geodetic incertitude: elastic dimensions and an area that varies with each official source. It fares best on the Internet and in guide-books, with '11,300 square kilometres' in the *Rough Guide*, '11,295 sq km (4,361 sq mi)' on Microsoft's *Encarta* and 'around

Lagoon behind the beach at Tanji

11,000 sq km' chez *Lonely Planet*. More authoritative, the *Commonwealth Fact Sheet* gives a total of 4049 square miles (10,367 square kilometres) and the government's *The Gambia in Brief* 4045 square miles (10,356 km²). With its 4003 square miles (10,247 km²), the *Encyclopædia Britannica* further reduces the country's size. Which is the last thing it needs. Whatever its actual extent, The Gambia is easily half as large again as Lincolnshire.

The northern and southern boundaries, both with Senegal, are at their widest 30 miles (48 kms) apart. From this distance on the coast they narrow inland to fifteen miles (24 kms) – the maximum range, according to

Whitehall wags, of British gunboats on the river. State and river stretch eastward for 304 miles/487 kms (or 201 miles/322 kms or 288 miles/460 kms viz. the above authorities) as far as the Barrakunda Falls, whereas landfall in the other direction is in the West Indies, 3000 miles away. The last remark is not fatuous: it helps explain The Gambia's involvement with the slave-trade. Wind and water aided and abetted: the Canary current carried ships from Europe south to the mouth of the river. While the doldrums then impeded their further passage around Africa, the north equatorial current and the prevailing north-east trade winds (not named that for nothing) combined to assist them across the Atlantic.

Venturing southward beyond Cape Non ('No further'), European navigators faced the flat inhospitable coast of the Western Sahara and Mauritania, 1100 miles with little water and few natural harbours, until the Senegal, Gambia and Casamance rivers were reached. All three rise in the Guinea plateau of Futa Jallon, the Gambia twelve miles from the 'town' of Labe. From here the distance to the sea is as the crow flies 150 miles, to the actual estuary about 300, but the river's meanderings protract its total length to over 1000 miles.

In The Gambia, the river's initial width of 600 feet is constricted to a twenty-foot channel by the Barrakunda Falls. For most writers these ledges of laterite rock are an 'obstacle to navigation': the presentday scarcity of boats above Fatoto makes the comment academic. For The Gambia the falls' significance is as the country's easternmost limit, below which the river is tidal. Koina is the first 'port' (viz. rickety jetty), Kristi Kunda ('Christ's Place') the first, now-defunct Anglican mission. At Fatoto is the first (small-dinghy) ferry.

Here the picturesque riverbanks impress with an average height of 40 feet, which varies with the rainfall and the tide. They illustrate how for the last one million years the river has gouged its course through the tertiary sandstone of the Senegambian plateau. Islands of harder ironstone

Flooded banto faros, near Farafenni

Air-roots of the mangroves, along any bolong

and gneiss have resisted erosion and now stand as isolated, flat-topped hills; pockets of kaolin supply the cottage-potteries near Basse. From here to the Atlantic, on terra firma everywhere, the topsoil is in general red laterite, an infertile 'ferruginous crust' that frustrates farmers but, like East Africa's murram, makes good 'roads'. It covers all too much of the country and, on any dry-season drive, the wayside vegetation, your vehicle and you.

A Barrakunda-like formation, the Buruko Rocks, again constricts the river. Squeezed into a channel only 100 feet wide, the faster current sweeps with it a mass of silt and sand; this alluvium removed in the upper reaches reforms as islands in the rambling middle river. Below Janjangbure (the late MacCarthy Island) they are named either from their part-extinct fauna – Baboon, Bird, Deer and Elephant – or, with many an alias, in the vernacular: Kai Hai, Pasari, Pasul and Pappa, Njubdu and Dankunku. Human habitation consists of Janjangbure (Georgetown) on the same-named island and, on the Baboon Islands, the national park wardens in remote confinement and the occasional privileged visitor to a study-group of chimpanzees.

The river's meanderings round these sometimes waterlogged obstacles meant 80 miles of difficult tacking in the days of sail: only with the advent of steam could Georgetown be easily reached and developed. Kuntaur is the all-time limit for ocean-going vessels and marks the

Timeless in The Gambia, a dig-out on the river

approximate point at which salinity yields to fresh water. (Salt water, to be precise, reaches in the dry season 140 miles up stream, and half that far during the rains.)

In riverside clearings decrepit piers step from the water to narrow mud causeways that run straight to villages built high and dry behind. These stand on slight rises, amidst the *banto faros*. Meaning in Mandinka 'beyond the swamp', these grasslands, often flooded by river and rain, are for the rest cultivable if salinity permits. In its final 93 miles below Elephant Island the broader, straighter river sidles off into larger creeks, here called bolons/bolongs. Many, like the

A groundnut cutter tacks up stream

largest Bintang Bolong, straggle north or south into Senegal; tortuous tributaries, they contribute fresh water when replenished by rain. Their banks, like those of the mainstream, are a tangle of mangrove swamps: not the Indian Ocean's lowly growth but off-shore forests in which air-roots arc symmetrically high and timber-straight trunks stand 60 feet tall.

As fertility deteriorates towards the river mouth – clay alluvium and sand predominating – the Gambia grows busier and more magnificent. Fishermen cast hand-nets from mahogany dug-outs and painted-plank pirogues. Tugs chug down in season with lighters of groundnuts in tow. Birds, as everywhere, astonish at every turn and dolphins frolic or bask like shark as you sail by.

En route you pass, as did the earliest settlers, two islands of not alluvium but rock. If the river is the axis round which the country's life turns, James Island was for centuries the hub. Dog Island, down stream, was first manned by Britain in 1661. St Andrew's/James Island – in mid-river, more extensive and defensible – had been frequented by the Portuguese since 1456. And sailing in untroubled by sandbanks or reefs (the estuary's bar is navigable and in the river's silt no coral grows), Hollanders, Frenchmen and the Duke of Courland's Germans had fought with them and died for these petty arid outcrops.

On the last and largest island stands the capital, Banjul. Despite a swampy, once-waterlogged site which, in Sir Richard Burton's words, was 'selected for proximity to mud, mangoes, malaria and miasma', Britain in 1816 established colonial Bathurst. From twelve miles at its widest, between Cape St Mary and Buniada Point, the Gambia estuary narrows here to under three. Thus initially of strategic importance, the new capital acquired both commercial and administrative significance as the British colony/protectorate took shape. Finally demarcated in 1889, that shape prompted the Victorian comment that 'its very appearance on the map is an invitation to the zealous reformer'. American journalists prefer the analogy of 'a long crooked finger poked into Senegal'.

Crossing the Gambia by ferry at Farafenni, the Trans-Gambia Highway is Senegal's strategic link between its capital, Dakar, and the Casamance

Sunset at Tendaba (inset)

limate

Weather-wise,
The Gambia is
Europe's antipodes,
Britain's better half

In September or October here the rains ease off and there starts a sunny season that lasts until April or May. Sea-breezes (the north-east trade winds) keep temperatures on the coast at an equable and pleasant average of 24°Centigrade/76° Fahrenheit. During the eight-month tourist season the thermometer drops to December, with the last 30 years' median *minimum* of 16°C/61°F. From January to May it climbs back to the October-November peak, measured over the same period as a *maximum* 32°C/91°F. At this time of year humidity is at an ideal 50-60%. Days are warm and nights cool.

which induces the south-west monsoons. Blowing from the ocean, these arrive laden with rain. In their first encounter with the weakening north-east trades (what scientists call the Inter-tropical Front) they deposit it on The Gambia in spectacular storms and tornados. (Wind and water have similar confrontations: when the cool Canary

The Gambia teeters climatically on the edge of the arid Sahel zone. The coast generally benefits from the ocean's tempering effect, but inland the Atlantic's sphere of influence is soon replaced by the Sahel's. The heat increases as humidity and even visibility drop. Especially when the north wind blows – the hazy *harmattan*, between February and May, for a week or two at a time – throats parch, lips crack and static is crisp in the atmosphere. Sensitive skins inland need dowsing with moisturizer. At such times the baobab tree prevents loss of water by shedding its leaves: man's only recourse is drink.

A word about the wet season may be of deterrent interest. As every A-level pupil knows, the air in the Sahara rises with the heat of summer, causing an area of low pressure

After August rains, on Jinack Island (left) and the Wassu 'road'
Tendaba sundowner (centre)
Offloading a cutter at Oyster Creek (opposite)

current meets the warmer Guinea stream, fogs occur off the Senegambian coast.) As the monsoons set in, ousting the trade winds between May and August, the rainfall is welcome but variable in force. While regular short showers leave clear skies, cloudbursts bring inches in minutes (or, as in August 1999, last hours and cause catastrophic damage). Though the sand and permeable soils drain too fast for streams and pools to survive for long, the vegetation then is at its most luxuriant. Nature-lovers not averse to sustained rain enjoy this season best.

The Gambia is lacking in mineral resources. The gold-mines for which it enjoyed chimeric fame have proved as elusive as the Philosopher's stone; ilmenite workings have been abandoned; the 'immense deposits of iron ore on the cliffs overhanging the river' are exploited only by armchair geographers, and salt – dried from the shallows and bolongs and packed in roadside baskets for transportation to market – is the only claim to geological wealth.

Agriculture

The rainfall during the monsoon season is a *sine qua non* for The Gambia's farmers, whose bane is its unpredictable start and finish, its occasional failure to appear at all or, as in 1999, its calamitous excess. Farming is none the less the nation's mainstay, accounting for 60% of per capita income and, with fishing, 74% of the work-force.

The varied topography described above – rich banto faros subject to floods, light sandy soils vitiated by salinity, fertile river silt often clogged with laterite – has as much effect as the climate on crops. The principal of these are groundnuts, rice and cotton, maize, millet and sorghum, market-garden produce and sesame, recently introduced.

Groundnuts are the corner-stone of agriculture, the economy and, in a sense, The Gambia itself. Known as *tio* in Mandinka, the 'peanut' or 'monkey nut' is the country's only significant export and principal cash crop. So vital are the unsightly swellings on the roots of this legume that books like Lady Southorn's *The Gambia* are subtitled *The Story of the Groundnut Colony*. And when that colony became independent the plant was chosen to top its coat of arms, which featured *dibongo*s and *dabandingo*s, the coop coops/hoes used to till it.

The Portuguese in the 16th century introduced the species from Brazil; the Gambians until the 1830s cultivated it for their own consumption only. Several odd quirks of colonial history were to be the cause and effect of its rapid development. Soap came into fashion in France (more so, it seems, than in Britain) and demand for groundnuts as its raw material grew: from 100 baskets in 1830 to a record 8636 tons in 1848. Soon overtaking hides, ivory and beeswax, the crop constituted by the 1850s over two thirds of the colony's export total. Production increased with Britain's colonial commitment. Agricultural advisers brought in new strains like the Rio Fresco/Rufisque, spread the use of fertilizers and implemented 'oxenization', prevailing upon villagers to use animals in lieu of the coop coop. By resisting the enticement to mechanize – tractors break down – The Gambia was able to progress simply while other African projects like Tanganyika's Groundnut Scheme turned into costly fiascos.

For three pence (50 bututs) the women on sidewalks and in market-places everywhere will measure you out, from their cheap Chinese bowls, a tomato puree tinful of crisp fresh-roasted nuts. Such 'Hand Picked Selected' and 'Philippine Pinks' may still be grown 'exclusively for the confectionery trade' but peanuts, neat, have long been of less importance than the oil pressed from them. The basis for French soap and the crop's initial success, this side-product soon so dominated the market that already in the 1860s Gambian nuts were hit by competition from American petroleum and 'belmontine'. After the Second World War, the Tanganyikan scheme had been designed to relieve a worldwide shortage of margarine; edible oil from Senegambian groundnut kernels, refined without odour or taste,

fights a losing battle with olive-oil on the European market. Partly to reduce our dependence on petroleum, partly to avert a produce 'mountain' (caused by the USA, West Africa and India), American scientists are looking to the groundnut as a source of new foodstuffs and ersatz petrol, paper, cosmetics and even industrial diamonds.

The farmers up river would be flattered if they knew. Each season they clear the bush where necessary in the time-honoured African way, by the ubiquitous 'slash and burn' technique. Joined seasonally by 'strange farmers' – share-cropping *nawettanes* from Mali, the Guineas and Senegal – they brush the fields ready for the first soil-softening

rain. They sometimes fertilize, then they (or more often now their oxen) plough. Planting takes place at the start of the monsoon; weeding is easy (which may be why this is all-male work) and picking begins as the wet season ends (given the requisite 750mm of rain and a minimum temperature of 24°C). After two or three seasons of this, and a one-year sortie into cereals, natural nutrients in the sandy soil are exhausted and the land, if not fertilized, should be left to lie fallow and revert to bush.

The plants are laid to dry on platforms, raised and covered to safeguard them respectively from vermin and belated rain. The villagers next beat the nuts free with forked sticks; they

'winnow' them either in loose-meshed panniers or in the rotating *passoires*, the long perforated cylinders seen in many villages. Collected and piled in open-air *seccos* or the larger centres' hangar-like 'bins', then graded, weighed and transported by lorry or lighter, 'quality' nuts – from December to March – should go for decortication at Kaur or Banjul; to these towns' wharves for direct shipment overseas or, for crushing into oil and 'cake', to Banjul's Denton Bridge.

For generations groundnut growers here had been an unwitting object-lesson for Rabelais' *Discourses in the Praise of Borrowers and Lenders*. The need to feed families through each

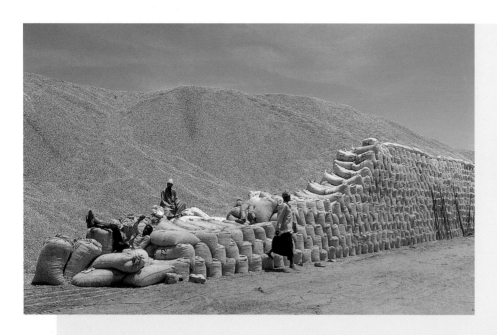

The Gambia and Senegal were still the world's largest commercial producers of groundnuts.

All this is history. Bankrupted by mismanagement and a slump in world market-prices, the board was privatised as the Gambia Groundnut Corporation, which was itself shut down by presidential decree in 1999. With this, the principal vehicle of the country's main crop, removed; with the IMF reducing aid pending a solution, and with fields flooded by exceptional rains in 1999, the immediate future for The Gambia's groundnuts looks bleak.

year's rainy season, to buy seed for sowing and to wait months for any return had made them dependent on advances of food and/or funds. Crop failure put them irretrievably in debt: to pioneer French firms like the CFAO, Maurel Frères and (until 1978) Maurel & Prom, to Lebanese traders and less scrupulous 'julamen' – Mungo Park's *Juli* – lending at 100% plus.

To keep hungry growers from eating the seed-nuts, and reducing the crop by picking prematurely for the sake of an early return, the colonial government in 1903 stepped in to subsidize, store and distribute. Which resulted simply in a transfer of the farmers' debt from the dealers to HMG. Owed £50,000 by 1921, Britain altered course. In 1924 an Agriculture Department was started, later a programme of expatriate advisers and local extension workers to organise seed-storage on a village basis, to encourage mixed farming and – the most far-reaching move – to form co-operatives.

The Gambia Co-operative Union lived longest of the many well-meant initiatives taken for the sake of the groundnut in recent years. After drought

in the early 1960s, better harvests and higher world prices helped The Gambia survive, against expectations, following independence in 1965. In 1973 the Gambia Produce Marketing Board took over the crop (like that of palm-kernels, rice and cotton), building depots, setting up annual buying stations, subsidizing fertilizers and holding 'price stabilization reserves'. A Gambia Commercial & Development Bank made the much-needed advances to farmers. The Gambia River Transport Company's seven barges provided lighterage at fixed 'zonal freight rates'. In the 1980s

Besides giving front-page prominence to the groundnut 'results', Banjul's letterpress dailies used to exhort readers to 'Light up with Briquettes'. This solid fuel, from compacted groundnut-shells, was sold cheaply in lieu of the charcoal with which too many village housewives cook and heat. (Hoardings around Banjul announcing the 'EEC/Sahel Butane Gas Programme' are all that survives of a similarly short-lived alternative.) For charcoal-makers cut and burn whole forests, destroying the habitat of many wildlife species and also the vegetation cover. This causes steady desertification and The Gambia, like many African states, has banned random charcoal-burning. The sack-loads seen for sale by roadsides now should have been brought in from the Casamance.

The need to conserve the oil-palm explains the attempted prohibition of another once-popular product: palm-toddy. Bainunka men, especially in the Kombos, you can still see scaling the footholed trunk with their fixed elliptical sling, the *kajandak* resembling a windsurfing boom. They tap the tree just below the flower-stalk, fill a gourd or two and, lax Muslims, sell off what little they leave unconsumed of the fast-fermenting liquor. (A dance done by Jola women depicts *Cassa*-tappers in their *daaka*, palm-wine

Palms, and palm-wine tapper

'brewery'.) Strictly, only small-time tapping is allowed now, just enough to jollify friends and family. For removal of the sap not only impairs the oil, it has also made of the palm itself an endangered species. Some fruit is boiled and crushed, the palm-oil you taste in local dishes exuding from the flesh, the mesocarp. But the oil from the kernels being worth more, these were in better times bagged for export to Europe.

Longer heads have always thought that The Gambia's reliance on the 'cash monoculture' of groundnuts was unwise. The alternative, or rather adjunct, of cotton has often been mooted – especially in the 19th century when Americans were prospering on southern plantations and Victorian Britain, rich from India, was turning Egypt from self-sufficiency in wheat to dependence on international cotton-price fluctuations. Here the crop has a long and chequered history. Reaching the Gambia in 1455, the

Portuguese explorer Luiz de Cadamosto was 'astonished to find the inhabitants clothed'. For centuries the Serahulis, Fulas and Mandinkas had grown 'tree cotton' from which to make the *pagnes* they dyed with indigo (the secret of weaving, so they say, having come from a fisherman who learned it from a jinn). In 1760, impressed by Senegambian samples, the London Society of Arts had offered a gold medal for the importer of the greatest quantity, 'not less than two tons', but only in 1833 was that amount attained. Settling the Liberated Africans up river, the 'Home Government' in London supplied them with Sea Island cotton-seed. An official report of 1860 gave 206 tons as grown and traded annually: 'If cultivation . . . is now taken up seriously,' it said, 'the export return should shortly become substantial'. 'Shortly' was not until 1904, when 70 tons left Bathurst for London. There the British Cotton Growing Association had been set up in 1902; in 1903 £500,000 were found for advances to planters and experimental farms, for seed, ginneries and baling machines; King Edward in 1904 gave his blessing by way of a Royal

Ample manpower and scant funds means more manual labour than mechanization (right) Picking cotton near Basse (below)

Charter . . . and in 1906 all Bathurst could report was that 'cotton might be taken up . . . if it is seen to pay'.

Replacing the endemic 'tree' with hardier 'hairy' cotton, planters moved to Nigerian varieties then settled on 'American Upland'. Ploughing and harrowing for sowing must be deep. Sowing must be done by hand, in precisely the right week or two, with the soil just sufficiently moist. No moisture must touch the bolls during picking . . . Growing only on the well-drained sandy soils of the middle and upper river, where groundnuts also fare best (and require much less effort of the selfsame workforce), cotton looked likely to remain for some time a perenially 'promising' crop.

That The Gambia's cotton has not gone the way of its groundnuts is due to the *Compagnie française pour le Développement des Fibres textiles*. Established in Paris in 1948 and now operating in most of Africa's cotton-growing countries, the CFDT in 1992 established with the Gambian government the Gambian Cotton Company, GAMCOT. In a project financed by the French and Gambian govern-

Traditional weaving at a *bengdula*, craft market
Rice-paddies, women's work (opposite)

ments, growers are supplied with insecticides, implements, fertilizer and seeds on credit. The hub of this joint enterprise is the Basse ginnery: the lorryloads of seed cotton delivered from local growers, and north-west Guinea's, are here reduced to lint (the seeds left going for cattlefeed or oil), then roadfreighted to Banjul for export. After disappointing crops in 1998 and '99, an optimistic GAMCOT manager in Basse hopes for an annual export average of 1500 tonnes of cotton lint.

Rubber and gum are bygones. Exports of the former stopped in 1901, 'no doubt because . . . the trees, not being judiciously tapped, withered and died'. The rubber-trees seen nowadays – *Funtumia elastica* or imported *Ficus elastica* – are ornamental relics. Humble gum (*gomme arabique*) became a Franco-British *casus belli* in the 18th and 19th centuries, when each country's African Company took up arms over this bacterial pus of the *Acacia senegalensis*. In moments of truce they traded the commodity for slaves: 360,000 pounds of the one for 100 of the other 'in their prime'. So important was the gum of Portendic that, although in 1783 all Senegal was surrendered, British rights to the trade were conceded by the French (who demanded

and obtained in return the enclave of Albreda). Contending nevertheless with French seizure of their ships and sabotage of supplies, Bathurst's merchants maintained the commerce until in 1857 Albreda and the rights at Portendic were re-exchanged.

Rice, short grained, is a staple of long standing. As its cultivation needs care, men entrust it to the women. Traditionally they have utilized the upland areas where the banto faros are no longer too salt and the riverbanks not yet too high for flooding. Though covering only one tenth of the area under such 'rainfed' cultivation, irrigated paddies are the hope for the future. The men accept to help build the bunds, the banks of mud bound with grass around each paddy. The women plough; sometimes plant stake-fences to deter hungry hippos; transplant from the nurseries the six-inch seedlings, and weed – at the same time of year as their men tend the groundnuts. In December, with the waters subsided, the ripe stalks are cut one by one. Each day's harvest is then threshed: on the

ground, thrashed with sticks in the villages, churned in some centres' hand-operated drums or milled, in privileged places like Basse, by machine.

These techniques are basically Indian, but presentday Chinese were an obvious choice for advice. One of The Gambia's few memorials, by the south-bank ferry on Janjangbure Island, honours the Mr Lee who in 1966-69 led the first team of Taiwanese. These made way in 1974-75 for mainland Chinese (all of them but one, that is, who stayed on to run Fajara's Bamboo Restaurant). Sailing past Sapu, you still see perched on the river's edge the Chinese pumps which, with the first seeds, came free.

In 1973 the government's Development Project was started, and in 1984 the first harvest reaped at Jahali Pachaar. A showpiece of successful irrigation, the 3700 acres around these two centres promptly repaid a £23-million investment with a twice-yearly crop averaging seventeen tonnes per acre. This, to the amazement not only of its Euroconsult supervisers, was a rice output unparalleled anywhere in the world. And not since paralleled in The Gambia either.

There was momentary glory when Jahali Pachaar featured in *Time*, then a return to the customary gulf between planning and reality. An ambitious scheme to dam the River Gambia (to keep salinity down stream and maintain the supply of fresh water to the paddies) was dropped. RIDEP, another rice-development project, suffered 'changes in administration which created unforeseen negative impact'. And despite a further six-year plan – the Small-scale Water Control Project launched in 1991 – 'the most urgent concerns of farmers have not been met' (not least of which is day-care centres for working mothers). The perennial problems of rice-growing here are at present being tackled again by communist Chinese, their Agricultural Technical Mission providing advisers, machinery and high-yield seed.

Growing thickly on tall trees around Banjul, The Gambia's grapefruit and Java oranges are in spring a surprising sight. They are also for the most part pip (which is why the latter are usually peeled, sold off-white in the thick pith and just sucked). Limes are more amenable: a 100-acre estate at Yundum supplied for a while a factory producing 'single strength juice' and, from the peel, lime-oil.

Sheep and goats straggle everywhere, especially over your road by night. Their skins and hides, no longer wild animals', are a minor item on the country's list of exports. Odd domestic pigs are an unexpected sight around Barra, salvaging on sufferance amongst Muslim compounds.

Chickens were the victim of a Gambian fiasco to match Tanganyika's Groundnut Scheme. In 1948 Britain's Colonial Development Corporation allotted funds for a Mass Production Poultry Scheme at Yundum. An American director was appointed but his knowledge of local conditions was nil. Fowl typhoid in 1950 killed 80,000 chickens; the project depended on local feedstuffs which it proved impossible to find; Gambians objected that their short supplies of food were made even scarcer by the scheme, and in 1951 it was abandoned. Losses were £628,000: the 38,520 eggs produced had cost the British taxpayer £20.77 apiece. The late Yundum College was installed in the premises. The government has ever since left poultry to the private sector.

Raising livestock alongside crops was an obvious corollary to the government's encouragement of home meat-production (and of the use of fertilizers, since cattle in particular guarantee an instant, on-the-spot supply). Almost all of The Gambia's cattle are either zebus or smaller, tsetse-resistant *ndamas* cross-bred from the zebu and the West African Dwarf. The country's cowboys are for the most part Fulas, sometimes owning a few head themselves, more often tending the collective herds of others. They traditionally see their scrawny kine as a token of wealth, not a source of food. Though it could often improve the stock, they (like Kenya's Masai) would no more cull their herds than you would take three clean pounds for a dirty fiver

Vegetation

The agricultural décor to your travels up country is enhanced, naturally, by the vegetation. To the north of The Gambia, Sudan savanna deteriorates into desert; to the south, gallery and tropical rain forest engulfs equatorial Africa. The *cordon sanitaire* of these botanical extremes is formed by their lesser-scale counterparts: South Guinea savanna and South Guinea woodland. Ecologically the country extends into both, and its flora in particular is correspondingly rich.

Flowers are so delightful a part of the Gambian scene that only a botanical boor would dismiss them as mostly imported hybrids. Though slightly (and literally) gone to seed, the Botanic Garden at Cape St Mary is a rustic introduction to The Gambia's commercially cultivated species.

The hibiscus, dying daily, adorns most hotel gardens: yellow, orange, red, pink and white, 'Sleeping', Korean and the Japanese *Grandiflora*.

Bougainvillea, in the tropics and the Mediterranean area, is an unpredictable boon. In East Africa it spreads, entwined on wire frames, as a multicoloured carpet – mauve, magenta, mustard, salmon or white – but often declines to climb up or cascade down walls. Which is the only way it will grow around the Mediterranean, stockily covering vertical surfaces but refusing to grow low along the ground. In The Gambia it not only creeps and leans but also, as bushes, forms lengthy hedges: like English privet at Bungalow Beach or in solid circles of colour. The tamarisk, too, is clipped and trimmed into hedges.

Walls and corrugated-iron roofs are camouflaged convolvulus-mauve, with not convolvulus but *Thunbergia grandiflora*. The orchid-like Dutchman's Pipe climbs; Golden shower descends like orange honeysuckle. Convolvulus and honeysuckle, poinsettias, jasmin and sturdy oleander, night-fragrant *Datura* ('Angel's trumpet') and *Lagastroemia* ('Queen of the Flowers'), all flourish beside the jacaranda and banana-plant, its flowers weird-obscene, the long-podded flame-tree, and oddities like the Century palm which lives for 100 years, flowers once and dies.

Ground orchid & African crocus (upper left)

Thunbergia grandiflora (upper centre)

Golden shower on a restaurant pergola

Canna lily (left)

Natural forests have suffered, as everywhere, from the 20th century. One third of The Gambia's has vanished since independence, burned, cut or cleared for charcoal, timber or farms. But impressive patches survive: in forest parks which cover three per cent of the country and, easily accessible, at Bijilo and Abuko. In the latter reserve, lowlier savanna growth yields to closer riverine 'jungle'. The Grey plum's buttress-roots block the way like fallen trunks. Aerial and stilt-roots from the parasitic figs rise, entwined with dangling lianas. Tallos and Elephant trees ('African breadfruit') stand massive. With incredible foliage, the Cabbage or Candelabra trees add to the natural chiaras-curo.

Gallery forest in the Abuko Nature Reserve

The savanna, more widespread than woodland, is also less dramatic: low, loose-knit bush over which lone trees tower, grass-green in our autumn, parched brown by Christmas and often burned black in the spring. Scattered amidst the tracts scarred by shifting cultivation stand trees such as the Custard apple and the West African Gum copal; the African locust bean, the emetic Guinea peach and the much sought-after kola; the Black and the Gingerbread plum; ironwood, rosewood and Velvet tamarind; acacias like the fire-resistant winterthorn which, a perverse exception, sheds its leaves in the rainy season, and cassias like the West African laburnum, its seed-pods poisonous and its roots an aphrodisiac. (This last is local lore which I have not verified.)

Baobabs, on James Island (left) and *passim* on the savanna

The baobab, that tropical oddity, stands as the sentinel (or marks the long-gone spot) of every settlement. With boughs like roots, it is obviously growing upside down . . . doomed to do so, Africans say, because it would not stay where God placed it. They nevertheless make cold drinks and lollipops from the crisp white contents of its pods; grind flour from its 'monkey-bread' fruit; boil and eat its young leaves and strip it symmetrically, like cork-oaks in the Atlas, of the bark which is shredded for fibre.

The raffia-palm provides fibre for fencing, matting and furniture, sap for palm-toddy and polished seeds as beads for bracelets and ornamental knick-knacks. The rhun or fan-palm is easily recognized by the leaf-form from which it takes its name and from the standard borassus-bulge in its 100-foot trunk. Insect repelling and not rotting in salt water, this last goes into bridges, wharves and roofing, while lower leaves serve as fencing or poles. The Swamp date-palm prefers freshwater swamps, where it forms impenetrable clumps. Like the straggling rattan from which furniture is made, it is technically a vine.

The bamboo's 1000 species are the fastest growing of all living things, and 1000 known applications make it the world's most versatile. Here it helps bind the soil against erosion, and was widely burned until the recent ban – for charcoal, no longer as a cure for prickly heat. From the bamboo's stalk comes The Gambia's *krinting* which for walls and fencing vies with corrugated iron. The plant bursts into blossom only once, before dying, each decade or two.

The cottonsilk/kapok-tree dominates the savanna, in both abundance and size. The Gambia's White-flowered silk cotton is larger and more striking than its namesake in East Africa. Like the mango there, it often guards the 'village square': by the *bentengo* (platform) in the shade of this *bantango* is the *bantaba*, meeting-place. Buttressed by astonishing 'natural planks', its six-foot-wide trunk rises over 100 feet, providing a mass of albeit inferior timber for dug-outs, drums and not very durable coffins. From the seed-pods bursts the white floss (kapok) which fills mattresses, pillows and unreliable lifebelts.

Wildlife

With the Banjul Declaration a new concern for wildlife became Gambian government policy

Though the Gambian savanna boasts the tallest African trees, its surviving animals are, apart from hippos, smaller scale. The elephant, as collectors of colonial postage stamps know, was once the national emblem, and ivory was traded here in bulk. Since 1913 the only memento is the place-name Elephant Island. The last of the once-common Western giraffes was drowned near MacCarthy Island in 1899; in 1911 the last Giant or 'Derbian' eland was killed. The West African and the 'bastard' Korrigum hartebeest, the buffalo, Roan antelope, waterbuck and kob have all shared the same fate. Until very recently the odd lion was still reported regularly from Kuntaur. But such sightings were 'outstanding faunal events' and what features in an official picture-book as 'the King of the African jungle, and particularly that of the Gambia' was a domesticated monarch called MacCal, caged at Abuko and flown in from Longleat 'courtesy of British Caledonian.

On 18 February 1977, in what came to be known as the Banjul Declaration, ex-president Jawara's Independence Day speech pledged his government's 'untiring efforts to conserve for now and posterity as wide a spectrum as pos-

sible of our remaining fauna and flora'. The enabling legislation was the Wildlife Conservation Act which, passed the same year, outlawed hunting and the trade in animal products. A first reserve had already been established at Abuko in March 1968 and, in November 1978, five of the Baboon Islands were gazetted as the 1446-acre River Gambia National Park.

Although closed to the public, the latter remains better known than the two national parks and two reserves set up since. The Niumi National Park was created in 1986 and Kiang West National Park in 1987. Opposite the latter, across the River Gambia, the local ecosystem of savanna, salt-marsh and mangrove swamp has aroused such international interest that 85 square miles have become the Bao Bolon Wetland Reserve. Newest and most visited after Abuko is the Tanji Bird Reserve established in 1993.

MacCal, caged patriarch of Abuko's lions

Nile crocodile at Katchikali

The *éminence grise* of The Gambia's ecology, the 'saviour' of its wildlife in a sense, was the late Eddie Brewer OBE. Named in 1976 the first Director of Wildlife Conservation, he masterminded the country's pioneering programme and, answerable directly to the Office of the President, maintained its momentum until his retirement in 1990. His Gambian successor has benefitted both from a well-funded German forestry mission and specialized Irish support. Keen and competent, Irish-funded volunteers provide technical assistance and training to the Department of Parks & Wildlife Management. They have published a comprehensive guide to the country's protected areas and, to defray the high cost of maintaining them, recently launched a Friends of Abuko scheme to which your contribution is welcome.

While Eddie Brewer *was* Abuko, much of his daughter Stella's early life was devoted

to rehabilitating chimpanzees. Her protégés – first in Senegal's Niokolo Koba, later in the River Gambia National Park – were all first-generation immigrants, either confiscated from traders breaking the law or saved as orphans, circus-surplus or cast-off pets from overseas. They were for a while accommodated, pending transportation to the national park, in a 'rehabilitation centre' at Abuko. Nowadays the large cage there houses Patas monkeys taken from errant locals. The Gambia's last wild chimpanzees survived just into this century: so neither in the outback nor at Abuko will you see these tailless apes now. Nor indeed in the national park, where the 50-odd specimens of *Pan troglodytes* are safeguarded with justifiable scientific jealousy.

Read Stella Brewer's *Forest Dwellers* instead. The Russians paid more than for *Life on Earth* for the rights to this homely and moving account of her success in

Rehabilitated chimpanzees in the River Gambia National Park

training all-too-human chimps to survive in their natural environment. Filmed by Hugo van Lawick in 1976, the book takes her story up to 1977. An American, Janis Carter, has since taken over the privately funded Chimpanzee Rehabilitation Project, living devotedly and usually alone with the 29 original survivors and their score of offspring. Though one of her retinue 'speaks' sign language, she had also to practise and not preach as the only way of teaching: building and 'sleeping' on leaf nests twenty feet up; emitting 'good food grunts' and enjoying seeds and fruit; 'fishing' with a stick for ants, to be licked off and swallowed before they sting . . . but saved by the chimpanzees' unsuspected instinct from having to show them how to catch, smash and make a Chinese meal of other monkeys.

Red colobus, mother grooming

Patas monkeys drinking

Abuko's Western red colobus have also been the object of an American girl's PhD research. This took almost four years, and in a quick trip through the forest, savanna or swamp you should hope for no more than a treetop glimpse of these thumbless, black-backed and russet-fronted primates. Of the colobus' sixteen subspecies, the *Piliocolobus badius temminckii* lives only in The Gambia and Senegal, and in troops of 20-40 in which 'female adults are the most socially mobile' and 'males go out of their way to engage females in friendly behaviours'. Which may explain why in 1999 Abuko's colobus population was found to have been a healthy 122, and stable.

Callithrix is what we should now call the common Gambian monkey which, lately thought a subspecies of the Green vervet, has been accepted as a species in its own right. The black face is framed by a spiky white halo of whiskers; the belly is silver, the back olive-green, and the whole thing frequently seen. Rare on the other hand

Callithrix aka Green vervet

are the pink-lipped Campbell's monkey, formerly thought a subspecies of the equally rare Mona monkey (the distinct booming voice of which is probably all you will perceive) and the Demidoff's galago. Because of its eyes and nocturnal habits Linnæus gave the latter the Latin name for 'ghost'. Belonging to the Slow lemurs, from which we supposedly descend, the likewise nocturnal but common Senegal Bush baby is an evolutionary relative of man.

The Patas monkey's ability to run at twenty mph and its 'home range' of twenty square miles are the reasons why it so often frustrates photographers. Researchers into its feeding habits too, since each troop's treetop sentinel prevents any close approach, and the animals shot by villagers have all too often a bellyful filched from their fields. Aids to identification are the long legs, bushy eyebrows and dull orange fur.

The Western or Guinea baboon (*gong* in Wolof) frequents open country, with a few rocks for preference. A redder version of West Africa's Olive baboon, the Gambian variety – *Papio papio* – feeds mainly on grasses, seeds and fruit, though fancies on occasions hares, birds, other monkeys and crops. It seeks safety in numbers, of up to 300 per troop.

Lounging in the track ahead or loping off over the fields, youngsters clinging to mother's undercarriage while the maned and dog-faced patriarchs bark, baboons are for visitors a regular diversion. For farmers a regular pest. Never hunted here for food, they roam fearlessly close to civilization. They steer clear however of leopards, whose natural enemy (and favourite food) they are. Though still the sporadic cause of disappearing chickens, sheep and goats, The Gambia's *Panthera pardus* is as everywhere an endangered species. Nocturnal, rare and solitary, there is little risk/hope of your encountering one.

Hippopotamuses were protected during the British protectorate, with a £100 penalty for poaching. But barely 100 are now said to survive above Elephant Island. Here they surface – piggy ears and monstrous muzzles – to delight passers-by on their boats. And, if approached too close or escorting their young, also charge, ram and try to capsize them. The hippopotamus gives birth on land, suckles underwater and lives some 30 years. Though able to wander ten miles by night and even outrun a man, it rarely

does either as in places the banks at low tide impede it and elsewhere the riverside paddies provide the daily 300-400 pounds it must eat to sustain its two tons. Hippos feature larger in village scare-talk (and travel brochures) than real life: investigating farmers' complaints of their 'ravaging' rice-fields, an Oxford University expedition found only eight offenders in seven weeks of searching.

Crocodiles occur in two species here: the 'Blunt-nosed' Nile variety and the smaller, rarer, forest-dwelling Dwarf. The Blunt-noseds are those that pretend to doze by Abuko's Bambo Pool (*bambo* being Mandinka for crocodile) or splash disappointingly, leaving ripples on the bolong, when they see you too soon in your upriver canoe. They also tend to disappoint on the 'crocodile pools'. At Katchikali, Kartung and Berending childless wives, luckless wrestlers and unsuccessful businessmen arrive from distant villages – while tourists pay admission – to see the venerated reptiles. Visitors blanch as black pilgrims descend in the hope of being blessed with a sight of the Sacred White One. If seeing is believing, I have grounds for doubting the last. The odd smallish specimens that might deign appear will sleep on oblivious, jaws ajar. Or waddle off alarmed if approached by sceptical infidels.

Its ability to generate babies and/or business is debatable, but the crocodile proves its usefulness to fishermen by eating the river's predatory catfish. These it swallows fresh and whole. Small animals are swept from the water's edge by its tail, held under and drowned in its jaws, then hidden on the bank and eaten later, very 'high'. Plovers pick parasites from backs (not *pace* Herodotus, from between teeth), new sets of teeth grow until the age of 80 and the malignly primæval appearance is not deceptive: little changed since the Mesozoic era, crocodiles are sole survivors of the archosaur family of dinosaurs. Mothers lay and incubate up to 100 eggs, help their squeaking offspring break from the shells, then safeguard them, sometimes, from mongooses and monitors.

Grimm's duiker, juvenile

The tail of the Gambian mongoose accounts for half of the animal's fourteen inches. It is also long, thick and straight, not squirrel-bushy, on the country's other self-explanatory species: Marsh, Banded, Slender, Large Grey and White-tailed. Mongooses endear themselves to man, or to readers of *The Jungle Book* at least, by engaging snakes in lone combat. But only if given no choice. Normally they prefer to hunt in packs: for mice, birds and lizards by day in the savanna, or for chickens from compounds by night. Their numbers help distinguish mongooses from squirrels which, as in Europe, are seen at most in pairs.

Duikers are the charmingly diminutive, dainty-footed antelopes of which the Maxwell's species can be seen, almost tame, at Abuko. The Western Harnessed antelopes there too are 'inscribed' with

white lines on flanks and shoulders and patterned white dots on the rump. Formerly more abundant and trusting, they could in the 1900s 'be seen running fearlessly about the streets of Bathurst . . . a common feature in the grounds of Government House'.

The Western sitatunga, a semi-aquatic curiosity, survives in Kiang West National Park and elsewhere 'in middle river'. This antelope features less aptly in the Wildlife Department's crest since Abuko grew too dry for the five originally 'imported' there. Its feet that splay in water like a camel's in sand give the sitatunga exclusive right of entry to inaccessible

Spotted hyæna at Abuko

Warthog *alias* Bush pig

Western sitatunga, male and female

swamps, and make it a 'difficult animal to meet with'. It takes its scientific name of *Tragelaphus Spekei* from the Victorian explorer who, besides discovering the source of the Nile, first found it knee-deep in East Africa. Bohor reedbuck are still reported from the north bank, oribi in the west also, but neither in any number.

Hyænas are now known to kill for themselves and not merely scavenge. They do both neatly and hygienically, devouring even carcasses and so clearing the savanna of every last bone. In a consequently well-scoured enclosure at Abuko the multiple offspring born here of Buki and Buster, the first 'imported' pair, have an air of cuddly though

cringing domesticity. From the *Crocuta crocuta*, The Gambia's Spotted variety, come sudden unnerving bursts of the whiney-cackling 'laugh'. It has, experts say, possible sexual significance. In 1902 the colonial governor sent the London Zoo a Gambian hyæna which soon became the 'best behaved and tamest in the gardens'. With Dutch and Belgian participation, a hyæna breeding programme is a current Abuko project.

The warthog (by the zoologists' curious expedient of counting toes) is related to the hippopotamus. Its raids on crops are related to the authorities who issue hunting permits. (This only to certain vetted residents and usually in the dry season when lack of food elsewhere makes north-bank plantations attractive.) Warthogs/Bush pigs swim. They also grub up roots and crops (the 'warts' protecting the face?) and, when alarmed, trot podgily off, tail erect and family following in order of importance. The warthog is here called 'bush pig' so that visitors can confuse it with the African bush pig *alias* Red hog. No confusion occurs in local minds: the latter is too rare.

Yard-long 'iguanas' (grey-green and yellow Nile monitors) you may glimpse doing press-ups in riverside clearings or fighting the current across. (The swimming sinuosity also seen is probably not a Smyth's Water snake but the 'Snake-bird', the African darter.) Odd monitors

Nile monitor, alarmed

ambling arthritically across the gardens of the Bungalow Beach and Bakotu hotels occasionally cause consternation. Agamas, at their best in irridescent yellow and blue, more often sandily drab, are the homely and ubiquitous lizards which bask in hotel gardens. Unless you move smoothly into their circular field of vision, they scuttle off jerkily up walls. Outside walls, I should add. Inside, and even upside down on ceilings, their smaller relatives are geckos. If the ceiling in question is above your bed, console yourself with the thought that without these harmless, newt-like 'house lizards' the night-time insects might be a bother.

Rarely seen creatures are responsible for the most frequent natural feature of the Gambian savanna: blind, soft-bodied termites that bind the earth with half-digested cellulose to build the astonishing peaks, pinnacles, hillocks and humps of the 'ant-hills' everywhere. In an intricate subterranean kingdom the massive queen breeds ceaselessly until, no longer fecund, she is licked to death. The 'workers' that kill her also fetch each colony's foodstuff of dead wood and straw, while 'soldier termites' with poisonous glands attempt to ward off aardvarks, and 'fishing' chimpanzees. Weaver ants 'sew' with silk spun by their larvæ the leaf nests sometimes seen at Abuko.

While civet cats 'characteristically accumulate their droppings on or inside' a termite-mound, its ventilation holes are the favourite daytime sleeping-place of snakes. Short of prodding them awake or rummaging in cemeteries, there is little chance of your ascertaining that The Gambia has 33 species. Few visitors do: the average number seen is invariably nil. What startles in the undergrowth is usually a skink and, since opening to the public 30 years ago, the Abuko Reserve has never had an 'incident'. The snakes are to blame: common Black cobras, Puff adders and Green mambas could all paralyse painfully and even kill a child, Spitting cobras hit your eyes with blinding venom, but they always hear you coming and prefer evasive action.

The non-poisonous African or Rock python has been so hunted for its twenty-foot skin that only small numbers survive, far from man. The shorter Royal python is so called because of its distinguished markings, but merits more its nicknames of 'Ball python/Shame snake'. Attacked or just approached, it betrays its stately looks and asphyxiating strength: it rolls into a ball with its head hid in the middle. Though easily found by the specialist, most snakes thus show a discreet considerate dread of the equally

timorous visitor. They add to this negative asset that of positively relishing frogs. To find your frog or Common African toad – *Bufo regularis* – one guide-book advises that you 'look around your hotel garden with a flashlight by night'. Most of us accept the other evidence and stay in bed enduring the loud collective croak.

Butterflies seem far less numerous than flower-filled gardens might lead you to expect. Only Swallowtails, their 'tailed' wings distinctive, are perennial attractions. African Migrants, green-tinged white and three inches wide, migrate obligingly near hotels and beaches. African Monarchs are recognized by orange wings tipped black, and Blue or Yellow Pansies by spots of each respective hue on black or yellow wings. Trying to identify butterflies that mimic other species' colours I find frustrating.

The Conservation Act is why even butterflies offered for sale should be declined and, ideally, reported. More durable mementos but equally taboo are tortoise- and turtleshells: the former seen on village rubbish dumps, remnants of the Bell's Hinged tortoise, the latter where fishermen beach their boats, from Marine turtles caught in the nets. The Soft-shelled River turtle does not furnish such souvenirs.

There is a wealth of seashells. On sale at the 'roadhead' south of Kartung are splendid specimens of the ten-inch *Cymbium glans*, the 'largest of the genus and the most graceful', with grains of sand trapped in its salmon-pink glaze; of spiney-whorled *Hexaplex* and *Murex senegalensis*, vermilion inside when taken alive, colourless (like all shells) when collected dead. Pied crows here are as fond as your canary of the common cuttlefish – not a fish but the skeleton of the squid. The half round, half serrated 'sand dollar' found on beaches is the skeleton of the sea-urchin. The Gambia's cockleshells even make a versatile building material: mixed like aggregate with bitumen for roads, set decoratively in concrete paths and benches, used as insulation on roofs and strewn like gravel in drives and gardens. Plaster and building-lime also come from burned

oyster-shells. The piles stacked by roadsides, not only near Oyster Creek, are destined for this: they are not evidence of aphrodisiacs or pearls. Though despised as 'mud oysters' by hotel chefs, they make thick and tasty pickings, from the mangrove roots, for villagers and fishermen on the bolongs.

The daily catch of molluscs, Ghana Town

On beaches and tidal flats, sand-crabs discern you, ogling with their 'eye-tufts', and scuttle for the nearest hole. Fiddler-crabs teem on the mud at low tide. Initially alarmed, reappearing just as promptly, they are recognized by their gigantic *chelæ*. On the males one of these claws is even fiercer, to woo females and warn off other males. The low-tide mud of the mangrove swamps is also home for the journalists' 'fish that breathe and climb trees': the African lungfish was first discovered in The Gambia, on MacCarthy Island in 1835. It hibernates during the tourist season, buried in riverside mud. The amphibious mudskipper is a biological anomaly seen by riverbanks and bolongs, moving true to its name and even scaling the stilt-roots of mangroves.

No visitor can remain oblivious to the brilliant abundance of The Gambia's birds. British tour operators feature special 'bird safaris'; travel agents on the spot offer excursions such as 'Birds & Breakfast', and at several hotels there are resident ornithologists.

Species reliably sighted to date total 560, of which over 270 in Abuko alone. Without even leaving the hotel, armchair ornithologists can birdwatch by the pool or from the terrace of their room. Common Garden bulbuls wake them at daybreak (calling 'Quick doctor quick!' so anthropomorphologists say). Red-billed Senegal Fire-finches flutter and peck under tables, Cockney sparrows of Africa but dazzlingly male-red. Pure white Cattle egrets on the lawns, Fajara's Pink-backed pelicans, African swifts dipping over swimming pools, superb Glossy starlings and some 30 wintering species enhance most hotel grounds.

Sandpipers and sanderlings, turnstones, oystercatchers, redshanks, greenshanks and godwits wade along the water-line; plovers scurry behind the beaches while Pied crows and magpies scavenge them clean. Gulls and terns perch on groynes or bob, a white flotilla, in the waves. Gorgeous Blue-cheeked bee-eaters teeter beside Long-tailed shrikes on telephone wires round Banjul. Nearby Abuko's riverine forest is the haunt of multicoloured rollers, sunbirds and barbets, parrots, parakeets and many other species. Weaver birds and lilytrotters live up to their name in nesting colonies and on ponds everywhere.

On a cruise up river or into a bolong, pelicans paddle lazily clear of your boat. Or, flying gracefully, land clumsily, to roost atop the tangled mangroves like the backdrop to a comic-grotesque opera. Perched even higher, superb River eagles look down on them and you. Immobile on a lower stump, Pied kingfishers suddenly plummet, wings folded back, on their prey. Ospreys catch the eye with a similar distant splash. Its plumage the colour of mud, the anvil-headed hammerkop refuses to move from your track, trusting in the African tradition that to kill it brings bad luck. Heavy-winged herons – Black-headed, Goliath or Grey – flap off as you approach. Cormorants perch with wings ajar to dry, while African darters wriggle underwater. Up country you flush the Double-spurred francolin: marabous and vultures near the villages may spook you.

(Row 1: Left to right) Black-headed plover, Village weaver, Purple glossy starling (Row 2) Abyssinian roller, Blue-breasted kingfisher, Red-billed hornbill (Row 3) Northern carmine bee-eater, Northern red bishop, Yellow-crowned gonolek (Row 4) Pygmy kingfisher, Crowned crane, Western reef heron

Government

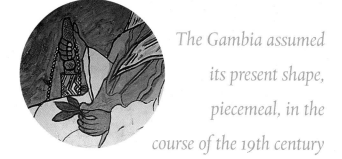

The Gambia assumed its present shape, piecemeal, in the course of the 19th century

The Gambia is an independent sovereign state, the sixteenth member of the Commonwealth and 115th of the United Nations. Head of state since 1994 is President Yahya A. J. J. Jammeh, whose Alliance for Patriotic Reorientation and Construction is the majority parliamentary party. The now-banned Peoples Progressive Party formed (as the Protectorate Peoples Party) by ex-president Jawara in 1958 won the colony's second general elections in 1962 and, with internal self-government granted by Britain the following year, led The Gambia to full independence on 18 February 1965. A second referendum in 1970 succeeded (where in 1965 a first had failed) in constituting the country a republic.

The headlines that in 1982 proclaimed the creation of a new state, Senegambia, were echoes of ideas 200 years old, but untrue. A British 'province' of that name was admittedly established in 1765, when the Gambian trading stations came to be administered from the Senegalese town of St Louis. It survived, though, only until 1783 when the Treaty of Versailles returned the latter to France. The Gambia and Senegal subsequently developed into distinct political and cultural entities, and their separate independence remains unchanged. On 1 February 1982 a Senegambian confederation came into effect: beside a projected joint parliament and unified foreign policy, Senegal was to benefit from a Customs union – The Gambia's low tariffs raised to Senegal's levels would have put paid to the former's busy transit trade – and The Gambia, having never had an army, had the reassuring presence of Senegal's gendarmerie.

The latter had been brought in to quell a first uprising in October 1980 against The Gambia's first president, Sir Dawda Kairaba Jawara. A second attempted coup in July 1981 was put down after a week of fighting by 3000 Senegalese troops (and the SAS). The leader of the insurrection escaped to Libya. The bullet-scarred reception of The Atlantic Hotel required redecorating.

The Senegambian marriage of convenience broke down finally when Jawara publicly criticized the union, and Senegal's president Abdou Diouf (needing the Banjul contingent returned for his conflict with Mauritania) abandoned it as 'a waste of time and money'. A notice in the Gambia National Museum records that 'In September 1989 the Confederation split and the Union of Senegambia was discontinued'.

Despite his Economic Recovery Programme launched in 1985, despite privatisation and a much-publicized but ineffectual crack-down on corruption, Jawara's popularity and authority waned in what the *Rough Guide* describes as 'a prevailing sense of stagnation and recycled rhetoric'. 'Guest soldiers' from neighbouring states, who had saved him in 1981, were to prove his undoing thirteen years later. In 1990 a Gambian contingent went with the West African ECOMOG forces peacekeeping in Liberia. The soldiers returned unpaid and, in the consequent crisis, the Gambian commander-in-chief resigned. He was replaced by a Nigerian officer and staff, and a defence agreement with Nigeria provided the military muscle which, despite re-election for a sixth term in 1992 and an amnesty for political opponents, Jawara needed increasingly.

Banjul's massive new monument has been named the Arch 22, the central park renamed from MacCarthy to 22nd July Square. For on that date in 1994 the coup that brought the present regime to power was apparently planned, implemented and completed. Gambian soldiers at Yundum Airport – turning out to welcome Jawara home, say some; returning from serving with ECOMOG, say others – were disarmed and humiliated by their Nigerian superiors. Disgruntlement erupted (aggravated by unpaid wages) and by nightfall Jawara, his vice-president and their families were safe but stripped of power aboard the *La Moure County* (an American warship which just happened to be moored off shore).

President Jammeh's claim that the coup was spontaneous and unpremeditated is lent credence by two plain handwritten pages exhibited in the Arch 22 Museum – 'Text of the Speech announcing the takeover of government by the AFPRC on 22 July 1994' – and a rusty-legged plywood stool labelled 'Chair. This is the chair on which

Independence Day parade in Banjul's 22nd July Square

the then Chairman of AFPRC and Head of State, Captain Yahya A J J Jammeh, (now President) sat … to announce the takeover …'. Jawara, who after 24 years in power had expressed a wish to retire, left first for asylum in Dakar then (having studied young as a veterinarian in Edinburgh) to quiet retirement in Sussex.

Following the bloodless coup (which holidaymakers here at the time are said not to have noticed), the 29-year-old then-Captain Jammeh introduced a military regime under a hastily formed Armed Forces Provisional Ruling Council. Recognition came from most West African states, including Senegal, while Western governments disapproved predictably. And, on learning that the AFPRC's 'provisional' meant four years, suspended aid. With

step, to Alliance for Patriotic Reorientation and Construction which (with opposition parties competing and not wholly unsuccessful) won the second republic's first parliamentary elections in January 1997.

Our knowledge of the traditional physical divisions of the country (into 'kingdoms' or, more correctly, spheres of tribal influence) is steadily increasing. Though some correspond to modern administrative limits, they carried little weight with the Anglo-French Boundary Commissions that in the late 1880s demarcated the presentday frontier with Senegal. Abolishing African slavery by the Act of 1807, Britain announced a first 'Settlement of the Gambia' as a base from which to enforce it. In 1814 the fort on James Island was reoccupied but in ruins, so two years later the

Chiefs (left) and members of the Gambian bar (above)

disorder and economic collapse threatening, and a counter-coup attempted, the Foreign Office in November 1994 advised that The Gambia was 'unsafe'. With most of the country's tourists from Britain, and most of its foreign earnings from them, this served to make matters financially worse.

President Jammeh's response was *Realpolitik*: civilian rule by means of elections would be restored in not four years but two. The Foreign Office withdrew its ruinous warning and tourists returned in a 1995-96 season that has been improved upon every year since. Jammeh surprised no one by winning the presidential elections of September 1996. The AFPRC was demobbed, in an acronymic side-

'king' of Kombo agreed to cede by treaty the island of St Mary's for the building of Bathurst/Banjul. 'King' Kolli of Kataba in 1823 reacted similarly to the offer of British friendship (plus a small cash annuity) and surrendered Lemain/MacCarthy/Janjangbure Island, and these two administrative/military outposts constituted the original colony. Brunnay, 'king' of Barra on the north bank opposite Banjul, was persuaded to yield the rivermouth's 'Ceded Mile' in 1826. 'British Kombo' (from Oyster Creek to beyond Cape St Mary) was obtained by treaty in 1840, all of Upper Kombo in 1853. The isolated French enclave of

Albreda was handed back to Britain in 1857, and various similar acquisitions were the missing pieces in the colonial jigsaw puzzle which constituted the protectorate.

Both this and the colony were governed through Sierra Leone until separation in 1843. 'Independence', with Bathurst's own 'Governor/Commander-in-Chief/Vice-Admiral of the Port', lasted until 1866. Then the rule of Freetown's Governor-in-Chief was resumed, The Gambia reincorporated into the West African Settlements, and the governor's burden of office lightened to simply 'Administrator'. Although Bathurst's legislative council was revived in 1888, it was not until 1901 that a governor was reinstated in the 'Crown Colony and Protectorate of The Gambia' – the state's official designation until independence in 1965.

The Gambia was in 1906 administratively split into five divisions which remain much the same today. The old South Bank Division and the 'capital and colony' of Kombo-Foni have become the Western and Lower River Divisions. The North Bank and Upper River divisions have retained their name and shape, and MacCarthy Island Division (despite its convenient abbreviation MID) was recently renamed Central River Division. Banjul has a city council, and in the 'provincie' seven area councils group the 35 traditional districts which each elect an MP to the House of Representatives and is each led by a *seyfo* or chief. Unlike colonial France, which installed French nationals or trusty 'natives' to rule, Britain preferred to enlist tribal worthies as agents of the central government. The once-hereditary *seyfolu* were thus left to judge local issues, with an *alkalu* (headman) as 'law-enforcer'… and still are, although to a diminishing degree.

Five Divisional Commissioners still administer from the same five 'colonial' divisional headquarters, but appeals from the chiefs' courts are nowadays heard by five group tribunals, no longer by the DC under a tree. Subsequent right of appeal, from the Banjul and Kanifing Muslim courts too, is to the High Court of The Gambia, thence to the Supreme Court. Thereafter only the president's prerogative saves murderers and rebels from the gallows at Mile Two. A legal system compounded of English law, Native law & Custom and Common law & Equity challenges and enriches the 80-odd members of the Gambian bar.

Rather like Spike Migillan, that well-known spelling error, The Gambia's name may be a mistake. 'Gambo', 'Gambra', 'Gamboa' or 'Gambea', the term had long been known to Europeans but not, it seems, to the Gambians themselves (who referred to the river as just that: *jio*, *dex* or

Playing at the opening of the Law Courts, Banjul

mayo in Mandinka, Wolof or Fula). The first Portuguese explorers, according to the griots, 'landed and met a Gambian called Kambi Manneh' (or, if not that, 'Kambi Sonko'). "What is the name of this place?" they asked. "My name is Kambi", he replied. They wrote that down'. The Mandinkas' pronouncing *g* as *k* adds some credibility at least. The guide-books' version of the place-name's derivation – from *Câmbio*, the Portuguese for (money) exchange – is not endorsed even by gung-ho Portuguese.

Kambia is a town in northern Sierra Leone. Gambia, they tell you, is preceded by *The* to distinguish it from this. And/or Zambia, since 1964 and the renaming of Northern Rhodesia. No one to my knowledge confuses Rutland with Jutland or Mali with Bali. The country and the river being 'ideo-inseparables', and the latter naturally referred to as the Gambia, I prefer the explanation of straightforward mental association between the one and The other. Acknowledging the article as part of the name gives it, like The Queen's College, Oxford, the right to a capital T. The only official exception was apparently the Anglican Bishop of Gambia and the Rio Pongas. Although recently updated to Bishop of The Gambia and Guinea, the designation still results in hoteliers requesting he take a double room.

Population

The above-average ratio of people to space is due more to lack of the latter than to over-explosive growth. The apparently high rate of demographic expansion – 4·2% per annum – is explained by immigration, mainly of refugees from wars in neighbouring states. They add 1·5% to The Gambia's natural increase of 2·7% per annum. Extrapolating from the last census total of 1,038,145 in 1993 (and by factors like 'Cumulated Current Fertility' and 'Mean Children Ever Borne' *sic*), the authorities estimate the population in the year 2000 to be 1·3 million.

The Gambia's ten-year censuses (besides enlightening elements such as 'Currently married/Ever married Economically active population Age ten years and over') enquire about Tribe/Ethnic group. 'Persons enumerated' viz. the Gambian public acknowledge themselves to be Mandinka/Jahanka, Fula/Tukulor or Wolof, Jola/Karoninka, Serahuli, Serer or Aku, Manjago, Bambara or Other Gambian.

Physical and facial traits are not so easily categorized. Travel writers talk of the 'slim athletic Mandinka with his fine and friendly traits', the 'tawny straight-haired Fula' and 'the taller Wolof, generous and intelligent, with an unnegroid nose and peaceable disposition', the 'blackest of Gambians' in one writer's view, 'lighter' according to another. Generations of intermarriage invalidate such facile aids to identification. Appearance, blood-ties, origins and religion have all failed to provide the ethnographic missing link. While 'British Indian' or 'American Irish' indicates origins (or clan associations), 'Scot', 'Yorkshireman' or 'Cockney' general habitat (or humour), West Africa's peoples move, mix and intermarry, frustrating the experts' attempts to define. Nowadays the latter take language to be the best criterion in classifying Africa's peoples.

Only those innocent of African orthography would attempt to list them alphabetically. 'None of these peoples had any script', wrote one colonial official, or at least only the marabouts' Arabic, and the compilers of the first reports were traders, explorers, missionaries and administrators. Scholarly consistency was not their forte; their spelling, like Lawrence's in the *Seven Pillars of Wisdom*, was cheerfully erratic. Mungo Park's Feloops are thus the protectorate's Floops or Felupps, *alias* the modern Jolas, Jolahs or Diolas. The Fulas are Fulahs, Foulahs or (in Nigeria) Fulani, the Mandinkas variously Mandingas, Mungdingoes, Mangdinkas or Mandingo(e)s. As for the Wolof, I am grateful to *Enter Gambia* for all the Rabelaisian possibilities: Woloff, Wolloff, Wollof, Joloff, Jolof, Jolloff, Jollof, Djolof, Jaloff, Joluff, Galofe, Yolof, Yaloff, Yuloff, Ioloff, Ouolaf, Oloff, or Oualofe. Not forgetting the Wallofs, Oullofs and the 18th century's 'Grand Jolloiffs'.

The Gambia's most numerous are those groups that speak Mande, a dialect of the Niger-Congo family of Bantu languages. Their homeland of Manding in the Futa Jallon explains the name Mandingo, their pronunciation the alternative version of Mandinka. Although one tradition has their king Amari Sonko conquering the future Niumi and Badibu in the 7th century, Manding or Mading is known to have been founded by Sunjata Keeta 600 years later.

Mandinka villagers wait for the river ferry

Manding/Mading is better known as the empire of Mali (or Melle/Melli), which in 1329 overran the neighbouring empire of Jenne (whence *Guinea*). Escorting the traders who fetched precious salt from the coast, Mali's young hunters then coalesced into an army that went west conquering an empire from Manding on the Niger as far as the Atlantic, and south from the Sahara to modern Sierra Leone. Only the *forolu* went to war, the highest Mandinka caste of the freeborn and sons of royal clans (assisted by their *jongolu*-slaves). Their social inferiors – the *julas* (traders), *nyamalolu* (artisans), Muslims and farmers – may not have complained about their exclusion from this 'noble' occupation.

By the 1500s Mali had suffered the fate of all empires, but the Mande-speaking kingdoms that replaced it maintained

slowly engulfed by Jolas and Fulas, they were largely demolished in the Soninki-Marabout Wars. It was nevertheless with the Mandinkas, wrote one stalwart British imperialist, that 'the English and French had chiefly to fight in their "peaceful penetration" of the Gambia and Senegal'.

The Mandinka proportion of the total population (39·5%) is declining nationwide but increasing around the capital. This finding of the census was surprising, for Banjul has customarily been predominantly Wolof. Colonial Britain furthered the preponderance, recruiting Wolofs (alongside Akus) into the Civil Service. The preference was slightly unexpected, for although some Wolofs had fled the French annexation of St Louis in 1816, settling with/for the British in Bathurst, their fellows in Salum and

a piecemeal Mandinka 'commonwealth' in the Gambia, Senegal and Niger river valleys. In the first, Kaabu was foremost. Flourishing under the Nyancho clan as metropolitan Mali fell, it perpetuated ruling families from which many a Gambian still boasts his descent. Only recently, however, has this early Mandinka nation come to academic ken.

In 1623 Richard Jobson's *Golden Trade* reported the Mandinkas as 'Lords and Commaunders' here still. Travelling via the Gambia to Manding, Mungo Park wrote in 1796: 'The Mandingoes constitute in truth the bulk of the inhabitants . . . and their language . . . is universally understood, and very generally spoken'. Their fourteen Gambian states had been mapped by Le Sieur d'Anville in 1751. Each ruled by a *mansa* (king) and council of elders (*alkalis/alkalolu*), they survived unchanged for another 100 years until,

Badibu were the spearhead of the Muslim revival which Britain in the mid-19th century helped the 'pagan' Mandinkas to resist.

While some trace East Africa's Bantus back to the Niger Valley, others reverse the demographic drift to explain the facial similarities between the Wolofs and the peoples of the Nile. Arab races, the 'Libyans' of antiquity, reached the Niger in the 7th century and may have sown their seeds. The Wolofs themselves stretch collective memories only as far back as Songhoi. From this 14-16th-century empire of 'Songai', 'Sanaga' or 'Sanagha' – perhaps established by Sudanese tribes and historically demolished in 1591 – comes the modern *Senegal*. There spelt usually N'Jay, in The Gambia N'Jie, the commonest Wolof family name is further evidence in favour of their claim to descend from the *Sungai*-speaking *Songhoi* colony of Gualata. Described by Cadamosto as 'Aza*naghi* or tawny Moors', the Wolofs called this homeland Gualafa, from which *Wolof* is a short linguistic step.

The Wolofs' documented history starts with the Portuguese. Colonizing southward in the 1480s, John II of Portugal gained a foothold in Sine Salum by offering to help one Bemoi against his brother Sibetah in a struggle for this 'Moorish', Muslim kingdom. Bemoi accepted the condition that he take up Christianity, visited Lisbon to be baptized by John, sailed home escorted by a Portuguese fleet and, promptly reneguing, was stabbed by its admiral. Seventeenth-century privateers suppressed mutinies amongst the 'Jaloff slaves'; in 1730 Francis Moore located in the Ba Salum 'Kingdom of the Grand Jolloiffs' the (still-undiscovered) Gualata.

Bathurst's Methodist missionaries found the Wolofs the most easily converted. During the Soninki-Marabout Wars, the predominantly Muslim Wolofs of Badibu and Bur Salum were decimated by their co-religionist Maba: in March 1863, 2000 refugees reached Barra Point, to rather alarm the one British constable on duty. (Outram Town, alongside Oyster Creek, was built for them and those that followed.) Few Wolofs resided hitherto in The Gambia's Mandinka kingdoms, but the half of Bathurst called Melville Town was already in the 1830s better known as 'Jollof Town'. The place-name, though changed, remains symptomatic: despite a decline from 52% in 1973 to 29% in 1993, Wolofs still form Banjul's largest ethnic group.

The Fulas come numerically between the Mandinkas and Wolofs. Their 18·8% of the national total is doubled in the area of Janjangbure, but the concentration implicit misleads. For the Fulas, though increasingly sedentary, are traditionally nomads and even, in one French writer's flight of fancy, 'descendants of the Shepherd Kings of Hyskos, driven from Lower Egypt sixteen centuries before Christ'. With straight hair, fine thin lips and a negroid coloration that could be called *fula* (red), the pure Fulani are an anthropological enigma. (Most young Fula women are undisguisedly attractive, and much sought-after. Many a West African man, dutifully married young to a family friend, neighbour or relation, aspires in later life to a second, Fula wife.)

Historically we know that the Fulas' ancestral home was Massina and the Futa Jallon. In the latter they lived pastorally alongside the Mandinkas 'with whom they had no quarrel, but even some affinity'. Timbo or Toobah was the Fulas' Manding, the 'seat of the hierarchy' to which, 'when

Wolof women (opposite) and griot in traditional dress

... about to make war, they send ... to invoke the prayers of its priests'. Their best-known collective and authenticated action is the 16th-century Great Trek: led by one Kolli Tengella (and guided by an oracular parrot), the 'Futa Fula' moved west en masse. They established the kingdom of *Fula*dugu, gave the Buruko Rocks the nickname of Pholey's (Fulas') Pass and disseminated the *Pholeycunda* (Fula Town) found *passim* on Francis Moore's map. Spreading north and west of the Gambia valley, they were finally contained by the Wolofs and, under the Denianke dynasty, founded the kingdom of Futa Toro which survived for 200 years more.

The 15th-century Portuguese had already found Fulas south of the river; their contemporaries are on record as purveyors of gold to Timbuktu. The warlords Maba and Musa Mollo were Muslim Fulas. Born in 1809, the son of a marabout in Badibu, 'Ma Bah' became the leader of the Muslim revival. With a Fula force of 3000 well-armed men, he broke the Mandinkas' hold on the valley and, until his death in 1867, led the British a bitty military dance.

Fula fire-eater in a tourist hotel

Fula schoolgirl, Fajara

In 1875 Musa Mollo came down from the Futa Jallon, to convert widely by the sword and found the kingdom of Fuladu.

The Fulas who in the 1850s moved down river to pillage (in a 'kind of annual outing', the *Official Handbook* says) were the Fulbe Futo from the Futa Jallon homeland ('Fulbe' being the term used by some for The Gambia's Fulas in general). The Fulbe Firdu and Torodo had gone before, the Fulbe Burure followed, and their divers offspring here now form the densest concentration of Fulas in West Africa. All that these 'Gambra Fuli' have in common is their speech (nine dialects of Fulfulde/Pulaar or Futa Fula, belonging to the West Atlantic group of Niger-Congo languages) and their cattle.

While the Fulas are multifarious the Jolas are fewer and more uniform. Their 10·6% of The Gambia's population is the tip of a demographic iceberg: the Jolas, Djollas, Djolas, Diolas, Dyolas and/or Karoninkas increase in density south through the Casamance, as far as the Ivory Coast. They are thought to be the region's aborigines but of that there is no proof: Western historians share the Jolas' ignorance as to their antecedents. The academic assumption appears to be that, as the Fulas, Wolofs and Mandinkas are known to be immigrants from elsewhere, the Jolas *faute de mieux* must have been here first.

The indigenous 'Floops' in 1447 killed the explorer Tristan Nunes, but later Portuguese relations with the Jola womenfolk were such that by 1700 their 'capital' of Bintang was 'chiefly inhabited by half-castes'. The Jolas were by then being forced west and south by the Mandinkas' advance, to be concentrated since in the district of Foni. In 1780 they housed and re-equipped a British naval force trapped by the French: '400 Jolas were mobilised to prevent the French from landing and destroying the factory of a British trader at Bintang'. 'English property, of considerable value, has frequently been left' there, noted Mungo Park, and guarded by the 'Feloops with the strictest honesty and punctuality'. Though some Jolas fought as mercenaries in the Soninki-Marabout Wars, their south-bank settlements were so ravaged by Fodi Kabba that sixteen of their 'kings' begged for British protection in 1887. And when his fellow warlord Fodi Silla was fleeing the expeditionary force in 1894, they loyally refused him asylum. The Jolas' escape route from these various marauders was from Foni into British Kombo. And even to St Mary's Island where in the 1840s they already formed a separate 'Jola Town' (and came to be called 'Banyons').

The unflattering comments of protectorate officials – that the Jolas, for example, were 'impervious to change' –

have been forgotten since 1994 when the regime was changed by a new Jola head of state. President Jammeh's attempts to mediate in conflicts in neighbouring Casamance and Guinea Bissau may have been prompted by the fact that both are predominantly fellow-Jola.

Next in numerical importance, with 8·9% of the population, come the Serahulis (*alias* the 'Serrahooli, Saruhele, Sarakole, Sera Koli, Serrekoli' or even, to Mungo Park's ear, 'Sierra-Woolly'). Speaking Mande, they are linguistic relatives of the Mandinkas but of older stock. Predating Mali and Gualata, Ghana was a 10-11th-century Serahuli empire that stretched, via The Gambia, from Mauritania to the modern state of that name. It was founded supposedly by lighter-skinned Berbers who thrived on trade with their homeland of Morocco. When their Ghana empire fell to Songhoi, many Serahulis moved south. By the 1450s they were well ensconced in the north-bank Gambian district of Wuli, where the Portuguese plied them with tobacco and strong drink. The latter may be blamed for some Afro-European interbreeding; the Mandinka kingdoms all around had a similar genetic effect and, on their Great Trek west through Wuli, the Fulas left 'the inevitable traces of

their passage, in the further mixing of the already confused strain'.

West Africa's upheavals in the 19th century brought further Serahuli immigration. Itinerant and enterprising, they served as mercenaries in the north-bank kingdoms and during the Soninki-Marabout Wars. Demba Sonko, for example, left the policing of his 'kingdom' of Niumi to 700 Serahulis under his son-in-law, Ansumana Jaggi. When Demba, 'a grasping old man', welshed on their wages in 1857, the colonial governor was obliged to intervene: settling the dispute at Fort Bullen, he repatriated half the force up river in the governmental yacht. The rest were permitted to cross 'in small parties' to Bathurst, where they were 'willingly employed by the merchants and traders' and subsequently given Kombo land.

The Serahulis nowadays grow groundnuts and, on their plots by Basse, The Gambia's best cotton; their womenfolk make pots in the villages near by, but one and all they are first and foremost traders. Their dealings enriched the original Ghana. They 'carried on a great commerce with the French in gold and slaves' and, Mungo Park continues, 'derived considerable profits by the sale of salt and

Southern Gambia and the Casamance, Jola griots

Aku mother and contented child

cotton'. With presentday interests vested more in Liberian diamonds and Banjul hotels, the Serahulis still warrant Park's verdict of 'indefatigable in their exertions to acquire wealth'.

The Tukulors (or Tukurols) are usually not thought an ethnic entity, rather the upshot of Fula penetration amongst the Serers in Fula Torodo. The Bainunkas too, though aboriginal, have merged in The Gambia with Jolas and Mandinkas, retaining their collective identity and matriarchal society only outside our area, in the Casamance. The only other groups acknowledged by the census are the Serer(e), Manjago and Bambara. The first, according to some, are 'relics of the primitive negro race which originally occupied the coast'. They may have been pushed down to the river mouth by Mauritanian Berbers in the 10-11th centuries. The Mandinka advances that sent the Jolas south to the Casamance forced the Serers back north. They rebounded south again in the 1850s, off Maba and his horde in Sine Salum. In 1863, 2000 crossed the river, to settle in Half Die and help construct the road from Oyster Creek to Cape St Mary. Their progeny are still found fishing on the river and farming in the Kombos. And on the bank at Barra building boats.

Like the Fulas, the Bambaras (or Vangaras)(or Wangara/Guangaras) sold gold to Timbuktu. Their warrings around Fuladu delayed Mungo Park and their general bellicosity seems, obliquely, to have benefitted Britain. By repeatedly raiding Kataba for cattle and slaves, they induced its king to surrender Lemain Island in 1823. Advancing again in 1840, they were frightened off by British reinforcements: a grateful King Kolli signed a treaty of friendship and commerce, ceded land to the British government and agreed to the building of Kataba Fort. In Ansumana's 'police force' was a band of Bambaras: while the British assisted the disbanded Serahulis, they drew the line at the latter and insisted they stay well away from Bathurst.

The Akus are interesting folk. Far from being autochthonous, they date their appearance in The Gambia very precisely to the 1830s. Or rather their partial reappearance, since they are descendants of the Liberated Africans. Britain in 1772 freed her 15,000 'negro servants' and, as a new home for 351 of their number, the Sierra Leone colony of Freetown was founded in 1787 by the Society for the Abolition of Slavery. The 'Abolition of Slaves' might have been a better title, for these former domestics of the British aristocracy found themselves 'deposited in good faith on . . . that brooding forest land from whence their forefathers had come'. Gentlemen's gentlemen, they were shipped to the sticks with, as their literal companions-in-arms, 60 women 'swept from the gutters of London and Portsmouth'. The unlikely bedfellows sired a light-skinned generation which moved north to seek a semblance of Britain in Bathurst.

Meanwhile the Royal Navy, armed by the Act of 1807, was intercepting the slaving ships: French, Spanish, Portuguese and particularly Americans flying the Spanish flag. Their human cargoes were recaptured and released, for 'rehabilitation' in Sierra Leone. And whenever it was Britain's turn to control that colonial shuttlecock, Gorée, she repatriated Negro slaves from this island-entrepôt to Freetown. They had been taken originally from every coastal region, and the Yoruba-speaking Akus amongst them explain the generalized name.

The first batch of Akus, 'of English extraction', had brought with them the names of their trades or adoptive employers: Coker, Cole and Forster, Turner, Wright and Joiner-George. Later arrivals looked to the Methodist missionaries, the Señoras and the Christian Wolofs who converted and/or cared for them – whence, on Gambian gravestones, such Wesleyan wonders as Wilhelmina Monday and Shiloh Emanuel Eagleton Joiner, and Catholic conceits like Victoria St Mary Chow and Josephine Alawole Lewis.

New Year's Eve 2000, parading the traditional *fanal*

With a lingua franca of English, the Akus were soon assimilated more to the British administration than to the native population. Their better education in the missionaries' schools entitled them to senior positions: if Reform Clubs are bastions of the Establishment the preponderance, by 1912, of Akus in Bathurst's is significant. Their influence waned with the British Empire; self-government in 1963 swung the vote away from their Democratic Party and undermined much of their political power.

Generally intelligent and good-looking, the Akus soldier on as a valued 'Western' element. In their wondrous Creole or pidgin English they pray in the Anglican churches and utter unrepeatable secrets at St John's Masonic Lodge. But their numbers and distinctiveness grow less. Few presentday children play with the Akus' traditional *gesse*-masks; some fathers try to Africanize the English family name, while more and more older sisters are adopting Afro hair-styles and dress. The increasing preference of Aku girls for Muslims should mean a next generation or two just as attractive but rather less Aku.

The Portuguese deserve a mention not because they survive in any number but because they were partly responsible both for the many coffee-coloured skins and for black Gambians named Da Silva and Gomez. Trade and evangelization were *arrière-pensées* of Prince Henry's during the Age of Discovery. But The Gambia sent back little gold, its kings were less interested in baptism than rum and, for the Portuguese settlers and crews, a more fruitful discovery was the womenfolk on shore. 'They are all married', according to Jobson in the 1620s, 'or rather keepe with

them the countrey blackewomen, of whome they beget children.' The south-bank settlement of Bintang/Geregia (viz. *igreja*, the Portuguese for church) was by 1700 a half-caste town.

Intermarriage (influenced by local matriarchal tradition?) had by then also resulted in that mulatto phenomenon, the Señoras/Signares. Roman Catholic, Creole-speaking and united with once-European merchants in wedlock or in lucrative liaisons, they remained the influential better half of Senegambian society for some 300 years. Many early travellers acknowledged their hospitality; succouring the hapless Liberated Africans, Bathurst's first Methodist missionaries received much assistance from this unexpected quarter.

Senegalese Señoras accompanied the French merchants attracted to Bathurst in the 1820s, where they fast acquired a reputation for ostentatious *chic*. British officials described with admiration (and clergymen with scorn) the Señoras walking out: their finery the latest Paris creations and their jewellery so abundant on their shapely persons as to overflow on to maids alongside. The Gambia's *fanals* (big, processional paper boats lit by candles inside) are said to have originated with the Señoras of St Louis, who had scale models of their townhouses made to keep alight the candles with which servants lit their way to midnight mass.) Though their bijous and their circumstances have long since been reduced, Banjul's Wolof women still make resplendent sights.

Syrian shopkeeper in Liberation Avenue, Banjul

Alex Haley in their yellow-brick depot that is now the Juffure Museum. And in 1854 one Monsieur Vermink began the *établissement* which in 1881 became the *Compagnie du Sénégal et de la Côte Occidentale d'Afrique*. The latter was simplified in 1887 to the *Compagnie française de l'Afrique Occidentale* – the 'French West Africa Company' viz. the centenarian CFAO that ran the biggest supermarkets in Banjul and Bakau.

The impression of Frenchness is enhanced by the Lebanese. The Gambia, so history books say, was 'discovered' by a Levantine. In his *Periplus* of 450 BC the Phoenician mariner Hanno reports 'an immense opening of the sea', on the shores of which he 'saw by night fires arising in all directions'. He took back to Carthage the skins of three 'gorillæ . . . of human form but shaggy and covered with hair who climbed precipices and threw stones'. Those eager to establish its historical credentials identify The Gambia from this questionable evidence of an estuary, the 'burning bush' (being cleared for cultivation) and baboons. Hanno, however, is now known to have deliberately misled: seeking new markets on behalf of a shrewd trading nation, he compiled his *Periplus* for the sake of a reputation, not to reveal commercial secrets to Carthage's competitors, the Greeks.

Whether or not these Phoenicians were here, many of their direct descendants have followed in their putative footsteps. (Until the creation of an independent Lebanon, the first to arrive were strictly Syrians.) In clothiers and grocers along Liberation Avenue fathers and sons take turns at the till. Handsome Levantines mend Mercedes and sell car parts by the main road through Jeshwang. The long-established Madis saw their oil-mill nationalized, but still do well on rents and dealerships for Nissan and Peugeot. The Milkys were pioneer hoteliers, running their properties with business-like *bonhomie* (until they were repossessed). Gambia Tours Ltd, which 'handles' Thomson Holidays clients, is the Lebanese Hobeika family's. Catholic, Muslim or Maronite, some marrying Gambians (and their numbers also swelled by kinsmen fleeing Liberia and Sierra Leone), the Syrians/Lebanese have for three or four generations been wholesaling and retailing, in three or four languages, with their famous/infamous flair.

British involvement in The Gambia has shifted in the main from governmental to individual. Independence of Britain in 1965 entailed relatively little immediate change in terms of personnel. The colony's Attorney-General became the late Chief Justice, and pre-independence administrative officers re-enlisted as contract or seconded

These fringe benefits of cohabitation came from living – on the fringes of Bathurst 'society' – with members of The Gambia's early Gallic community. After 200 years of rivalry with the French in Senegal (and despite the continuing 'intrusion' of Albreda), the British protectorate soon became the scene of a discreetly dynamic French presence. Reminders now are few – 'Le Commerce Africain' above a shack-shop at Albreda; a French grave at Fatoto; 'CFAO' still on Bakau's sold-off supermarket – but the Gallic impact was till recently important in The Gambia's mercantile history.

Joseph Maurel and Léon Prom moved here from Gorée in 1830 to set up a score of groundnut-trading stations. The firm of Maurel & Prom they founded abandoned that commodity in 1978; their Banjul base was in 1981 burned down, and in 1983 the cargo ships that bear their name made a last voyage up river. As the deeds to their original Wellington Street premises were signed by seven Maurels and two Proms, it is not surprising that the former should have gone it alone. Maurel Frères (not brothers but cousins of Joseph's) also ventured up river to buy and export groundnuts, branched into other lines around Banjul, and housed

Civil Servants. Gambia Airways, the airport and port, the ferries, the National Trading Corporation . . . many bodies both private and parastatal benefitted in the 1970s and '80s from British management and expertise. HMG's 'technical co-operation' officers included accountants, architects, economists, engineers and entomologists. Others were appointed to lecture, survey, nurse, anæsthetize, manage projects, process seeds and teach.

Such pride of place in the expatriate community ended with the Jawara regime: in 1994 all British aid programmes stopped. (Only the independent Voluntary Service Overseas continued with a task begun in 1960. Funded partly by HMG's Small Grants Scheme, it does so currently with some 40 two-year volunteers who, living in local housing, work at local rates of pay as doctors, nurses, teachers, accountants, engineers, librarians and business and community advisers.)

A half-dozen British technical officers stayed on after the coup, 'advisory privateers'. Six training officers have since been sent to assist the Gambian government with record management, transfer of knowledge and general good governance. This under an agreement signed in 1998 whereby Britain's Department for International Development provide grants of £9 million over the next four years . . . no longer to fund new public projects – 'No money changes hands' – but, significantly now, in Poverty Alleviation programmes.

A Caledonian Society (and a popular weekly 'hash run') thrive nevertheless. For the place of official British expats has been taken to some extent by individual entrepreneurs. From Bakau to Basse, English partners (in every sense) find themselves managing guest houses and local hotels. Couples from Cumbria or Cornwall run bars and restaurants. Seafaring Brits bring down their boats to operate river- and fishing-trips. These latterday settlers number 300-400, holidaymakers some 80,000 per annum. Though Germans have re-emerged *en masse* on the package-holiday scene, it is still the British that The Gambia attracts most.

The Holy Ghost Fathers and associated Sisters are a vital Irish and Canadian element, while a dozen volunteers with APSO, Ireland's Agency for Personnel Services Overseas, do sterling work not only in ecotourism and wildlife management. The Gambia's other white expatriates consist of a handful of brave Scandinavians who direct the hotels they built; of Germans, in travel, fishing and most significantly forestry (establishing the Bijilo Forest Reserve and spending DM-millions on combating desertification with fenced areas of woodland countrywide) and of numerous but transient Americans. None are old hands: the Catholic Relief Services came first in 1964, the Peace Corps three years later.

Like their British counterparts, most US nationals are here to aid and advise the deprived or undernourished: not members of AID's far-reaching programmes any more, but well-organised Peace Corps volunteers some 75 in number. Equipped with libraries and 'resource centers' up river (and each with a *Peace Corps Cross-Cultural Workbook*), they teach, train teachers and help with mother & infant care and increased crop production. The excellent CRS relies more on local recruitment. Anyone reading its Annual Report will not need telling that its origins, sponsors and directors are American. It 'articulates . . . a vision statement . . . for social upliftment'. But shows for all that a remarkable commitment to women's farming, child survival, adult literacy and 'a 2nd Track, Middle-out approach to peace building'.

Though rarely recognized as such by their white contemporaries, African expatriates predominate. Among the friendly and colourful crowds in the markets of Banjul and the settlements up river you see Mauritanians in their long, loose, sleeveless robes off-white or blue. (Bearded and Arabic-speaking, these lean and hollow-cheeked *Nar* seem unlikely scions of the Berber races whose onslaughts forced the Serers and Serahulis southward.) Up from the south, also understanding Arabic, Nigerians sell shells in Banjul's Albert Market, plus strips of hide and goats' horns for mixing native medicine. The blacks that address you in excellent French are not necessarily graduates of the *Alliance Franco-Gambienne* but either 'strange farmers' or out-of-work immigrants from Senegal or Mali. (With the unemployment problem hardly any better here, is it the kinder climate, or the tourists, that attract?) Likewise more fluent in French, many stallholders and shopkeepers are immigrants from Guinea. Places like Ibo Town and Ghana Town speak for themselves: businessmen from Ghana run the biggest fishery and Serahuli smugglers grew rich on Liberian diamonds – until these were replaced by refugees. Housed at the United Nations' Kerr Elhassa camp near Basse (and in the old Atlantic Hotel), fugitives from civil war in Liberia and Sierra Leone constitute involuntary expatriate communities. With fellow-refugees from the Casamance and Guinea Bissau held in another UN camp at Arankoli, they add 1·5% to The Gambia's population growth-rate.

Religion

*The Gambia is mainly
Muslim, increasingly
Christian and in
places tolerated
as pagan*

Lacking an establishment or articulate apologists, but indigenous-African, tribal-traditional and undoubtedly still widespread, paganism fares badly with official statisticians. In 1963, 29% of all Gambians claimed to be pagan. The census of 1973 dissected the population by Sex, Age, Tribe and twenty other attributes: 'Religious Denomination' was not one. As orthodox religion is known to have arrived here in the last 1300 years, paganism must *ipso facto* be the region's original faith. Usually euphemized as animism or fetishism, it long proved impervious to foreign persuasions and remains influential.

The Christian Portuguese made mostly opportunist converts: their churches at Bintang, Juffure and Tankular administered more to sailors and settlers than to Africans. Armed with papal bulls in favour of slavery, the Germans, Dutch, British and French that followed let drop any evangelical pretence and concentrated unashamedly on commercial exploitation. The creation of Bathurst and the British protectorate made for radical change. In 1820 The

Gambia 'was recommended to the General Wesleyan Missionary Committee as an eligible spot'. Two years later Mother Anne-Marie Javouhey, first of the Sisters of St Joseph of Cluny, visited Bathurst and planned a Catholic mission that did not however materialize till 1849. (A popular T-shirt in 1999 commemorated the mission's 150th anniversary.)

Catholicism floundered here for 50 years, most of its 'officiating Spiritans' (Holy Ghost Fathers from France) dying of disease before the age of 40. Arriving in 1905, the Irish father John Meehan gave the mission a literal new lease of life. It was detached from Dakar in 1931, promoted Apostolic Prefecture in 1951 and in 1957 made the 'Diocese of Bathurst in Gambia'. This *mutatis mutandis* is now led by five Irish priests, twelve Gambians ordained since 1985 and three Nigerian Missionaries of St Paul sent in 1992. It consists of some 15,000 souls, the fine cathedral in Daniel Goddard/Hagan Street and a network of countrywide churches and outstations that, numbering 45 in 1999, is steadily increasing.

In an intellectually admirable paper the Holy Ghost Fathers have assessed their past and present place amongst The Gambia's Muslim majority: educating, in their five 'grant-aided' senior secondary, five junior secondary and 26 primary schools; maintaining the dialogue 'Pro non-Christianis' and constituting 'the dynamic representative minority . . . spiritually responsible for all'.

Their Anglican and Methodist colleagues likewise apply themselves more to education than evangelization. The Methodists in 1821 rose to the call (above) and sent John Morgan and the ailing John Baker on a missionary reconnaissance. (They were, like a Quaker inquirer, recommended by the colonial governor to start at Tendaba, but the headman there reacted diplomatically by advising them to build near the river, 'then you can always jump into a canoe and get away'.) Bathurst's Wolofs and Akus were

Confirmation day at Banjul's Catholic cathedral

more receptive and, as the Liberated Africans Department settled batches of the latter up river, Brother Morgan's helpers followed in their wake. In 1822 Morgan opened Bathurst's first boys' high school. The girls' school founded in 1824 by the Quaker Hannah Kilham was taken over by a Methodist couple called Hawkins, and in 1835 the present Wesley Church was completed in Dobson (now Macoumba Jallow) Street. The educational cluster there still; the Bethel Nursery School beside the church in Stanley Street; the later, plainer chapels at Bakau and Serekunda, and Janjangbure's church and primary school are all tributes to the successive Wesleyans who rarely survived their tour of duty here.

Given the part of British officialdom in the early colony, the Church of England arrived surprisingly late. 'In fact it was only by accident that Anglicans came to be here at all', said the late Very Rev. J. C. Faye, one-time Gambian High Commissioner, minister of state and grand old man of pious establishment politics. The padre attached to the West Indian regiments here left when they were withdrawn, but the Bishop of Sierra Leone responded to the Bathurst merchants' offer of a stipend and accommodation by sending a permanent replacement in 1836. Only in 1901, however, was the Anglican cathedral of St Mary's completed. Its wall-plaques (many older and relocated here) show that it promptly assumed its rôle as official seat of worship. Some commemorate those who took 'decisive measures against the natives of Barra', were 'slain at Saba' or 'murdered at Sankandi'. Others are dedicated to 'Commandants of this Settlement', Colonial secretaries and Acting administrators, governors, travelling commissioners, naval captains and constables, and almost all donated by fellow officers or indebted 'directors and shareholders of the Bathurst Trading Company'.

The Anglicans duly contributed schools (St Mary's in 1939 and the Parsonage Nursery) and, remaining Aku-civic and close to the establishment, they like the Wolofs entered politics at the prospect of independence. In 1951 'Uncle' Faye founded the Democratic Party. (Merging with the Muslims as the Democratic Congress Party, this finally renounced its odd programme of confederation with Sierra Leone and bowed out in 1968.) Faye meanwhile had been headman of Kristi Kunda: its former St John's Church and Transfiguration School was the last, remotest outpost of the Anglicans' Upper River Mission. Their land at Basse was half leased off to the Standard Bank, half occupied by St Cuthbert's. The War-time hut at Bakau was in the 1970s rebuilt as St Paul's, and a mud hut thrown up in 1945 was promoted to Christ Church, Serekunda. With St Andrew's at Lamin and Farafenni's Church of the African Martyrs, the Anglicans share with the Methodists one half of The Gambia's Christian four per cent.

That this is only one per cent lower than in 1973 is, paradoxically, the sign of a Christian revival. For in that period the country's population has risen by 49%. According to pre-independence documents, The Gambia was a predominantly Christian colony. The records, inadequate, may have reflected wishful thinking in Whitehall, but the recent rapid spread of Islam over Black Africa is incontrovertible. It was also thought by churchmen to be irreversible. Converts are born not won to Islam, they said. With large families and several wives (the two factors not unconnected) the Muslim majority in an expanding population must increase exponentially.

The Christian minority has however defied predictions and is growing in numbers too. Well funded from Rome and private donors, the active Bishop Cleary may have brought about Catholic expansion, the Education Secretariat working with the government, the Caritas development wing digging wells, helping village women and combating adult illiteracy. But like their Anglican and Methodist fellows in The Gambia Christian Council, Catholics report 'progress slow or almost imperceptible from the conversion point of view'. For it is the breakaway African Independent Churches that have fuelled the recent revival. Preachers of 'holy roller evangelism', faith healing and 'prosperity theology' have won so many converts across the continent that the proportion of Africa's to Christians worldwide has doubled from one in ten in 1970 to one in five today. Christianity, according to *Time*, is increasing by 3·5% annually in Africa compared with one per cent in Europe and North America. Focused on The Gambia, this trend translates into many a popular new place of worship, especially around Banjul: the New Covenant Worship Centre, Deeper Christian Life Mission, Celestial Church of Christ, Apostolic Faith Mission, Assemblies of God in The Gambia, Grace Independent Church, Good Seed Mission and the 'World Mission Agency Winners' Chapel'.

Organizations like WEC International – the Worldwide Evangelization for Christ – combine hot gospelling with the mainstream churches' aid: staffing a half-dozen village clinics, running rural training centres and now IT courses too. 'Multinational' is no longer just a big-business term: WEC counts fourteen nationalities amongst its 30-strong Gambian team (it not being generally known that Korea is

Church sports day on Cape Point beach

the largest provider of Christian field-workers worldwide). And combining modern evangelism with colonialism's traditional *mission civilisatrice*, the CRS is first and WEC second in teaching villagers to read in the vernacular. Their adult-literacy campaigns are not disinterested: most of the vernacular (like the President's native Jola) has little or no literature, and the missions' translations of the Bible will be their pupils' only reading matter.

There is a Seventh-day Adventist Church in Kanifing; fetishism, we may assume, is the solace of a far more sizeable minority but, whether practising or lapsed, the Gambian majority is Muslim. They are technically of the Sunni sect, and Malikite tenets are applied in the Islamic courts. This for most Gambians, though, is the *Bourgeois Gentilhomme*'s prose: at most they avow themselves members of the Senegambian Tijani or Murad communities.

The first decades of British missionary effort coincided – by chance? – with a revival of Islam. The word of the Prophet had been heard here long before, Arab armies having reached the Niger in the 7th century. The faith spread with trade, through Morocco and Mauritania to the empire of Mali: in 1324-25 one Gongo Musa performed the *Hajj* (the pilgrimage to Mecca) and resided in Cairo with so impressive a retinue as to warrant a mention in contemporary Arab chronicles. The Mandinkas' dispersal from Mali to Kaabu was no doubt a fillip to The Gambia's Islam. Except amongst the Fulas, it none the less remained the domain of a chosen few: the marabouts, 'marybuckes' or morymen, whose literacy in Arabic was useful to unschooled rulers but whose proselytes were consigned to a 'Marabout's place' or *Morykunda*. In these satellite villages they lived safe from Soninki 'contamination' but within beck and call of their Mandinka overlords.

could clearly not be countenanced by Victorian Britain in a colony and protectorate. The Royal African Corps of 'blue-jackets' and marines, seconded West Indian regiments and the Bathurst Militia with enlisted English merchants received half-hearted help from Whitehall in containing the Muslim outbreaks. The problem was partly disposed of by chasing the ringleaders into French Senegal.

The failure of this Islamic revival, the British-backed success of Soninki animism is often seen as a reason for the relaxed, pragmatic tolerance shown by Gambian Muslims today. You may with impunity (and shoes removed) visit village mosques and backyard *jakas* (praying-places). Early Friday afternoon, dressed in their Friday best, the men of every hamlet start their walk to the nearest *juma*. (Prayers at the old Great Mosque on this Muslim sabbath caused Banjul's weekly traffic jam.) But devotions are affable, not fanatical: The Gambia's law is not the Shari'a; there is

Due perhaps to accumulated pique, perhaps to the appearance of more warlike marabouts, Senegambian Muslims in the 1850s commenced a series of bitty uprisings glorified with the title of Soninki-Marabout Wars. The Muslim warlords Musa Mollo, Maba, Fodi Silla and Fodi Kabba engaged bands of Jola and Serahuli mercenaries, plundered and displaced the Wolofs and Serers and destroyed the Mandinka kingdoms. Such disturbances

nothing of the blinkered and insidious Islam that taints some Middle Eastern states.

Only the lucky few can now afford the pilgrimage to Mecca. At Friday prayers the faithful are grateful to the many beggars: thanks to them another Muslim duty of almsgiving can be done. The month-long daytime fast of Ramadhan is generally observed, and the '*Ids*, here called *Koriteh* and *Tabaski*, are popular holidays (which cost

fathers new family clothes, and a sheep, and husbands new dresses and hair-dos).

Up country the *pickens* sit in the village square, learning the Arabic inscribed on wooden paddles. Older brothers, before and after school, attend the local *dala* to study the Qoran, the *Hadisi* (Hadith) and the *Sungna* (Sunna), the 'gospel according to Mohammed'. Nowadays the occasional *sering dala* even teaches Arabic as a spoken language, not simply as a vehicle of liturgy as was many Catholics' Latin. The marabouts, influential still, have reverted more to their North African rôle of soothsayers and purveyors of placebos. Famous morymen, often from Mauritania, pitch their marquees by the roadside in Banjul, to advise piously (for a price) and hold well-attended court like mediæval potentates.

Such visiting celebrities charge more than the streetcorner marabout for jujus. Amulets, gris-gris, the locals' *taami matu* (and derived from *joujou*, the French for toy), they are worn round every neck, arm, waist or ankle; simple bangles, *tafu* (neck-cloths) or scraps of paper enclosed

The new Great Mosque of Banjul (above) is named in honour of its principal benefactor, King Fahd of Saudi Arabia. Friday prayers, soon after noon, are the most important. Not only men attend, but women enter separately and pray apart.

in lockets to keep the name of Allah clean. They do not appear to be sacrosanct (Gambians hand them over or open them up on request), just indispensable. When Mr Morgan in 1822 asked his parishioners to take theirs off, they burned his Wesley Church down. Church outings are popular, said one parish priest, but not for swimming: undressed, the parishioners would expose their pagan jujus. On my first drive outside Banjul, three bracelets replaced the usual one on my driver's arm: he reported late, having had to see his marabout to extend his juju-cover for up country. Childless wives, unsuccessful businessmen, the sick and soldiers off to war all apply to their marabout for the appropriate charm to wear or best *naso* to drink.

The reasons given for their use of jujus are as many as the Gambians you ask. Theologians see them as indication of the Africans' hankering for tangible tokens of the supernatural or divine, their reluctance (or inability) to indulge in purely cerebral acts of faith. Scholars point to the Old Testament parallel of Rachel's stealing *teraphim* (jujus?) from her father, and Homer's having Ulysses wear a ribbon to keep him from drowning. Frank Catholics equate them with St Christophers on dash-boards and miraculous medals of Our Lady hung round necks. There may well be a connection: the renovation of the Banjul cathedral was an opportunity for the fathers to heed Rome's admonitions on the veneration of saints and remove most of the statues. But the congregation protested, turning out to light candles to such as the 'absent St Anthony'.

Friday prayers at the King Fahd Mosque, Banjul (opposite)

Ceremonial dancing amongst Muslim Jolas (above)

Jujus and knick-knacks worn by a Lebu wife

Those whose *balandango*-roots fail to save them from bullets rarely come back and complain; but others whose jujus avail them naught appeal to the crocodile pools. Or make a pilgrimage to the holy places, idyllic spots with pagan associations like Sanneh-Mentering, Tengworo, Kenye-Kenye Jamango or Nyanitama-Dibindinto. Dressed in their best and accompanied by the alkalu, suppliant men and would-be mothers trek from even neighbouring states to offer up prayers, plus kola-nuts, money, cloth or a slave. They may stay for several days, sleeping in the flimsy thatched huts, sometimes refusing food and drink, their devotions unorthodox but their piety impressive.

Dress

So delightfully varied is the Gambians' everyday dress that jujus might seem to be the only common item of attire. Only Banjul schoolchildren are brightly and literally uniform; only green (the holy colour of Islam) is not very commonly seen. For the rest, the array of fashions and shades is amazing; except amongst Banjul's bureaucracy there is no suit-and-tie or skirt-and-blouse conformity. West African apparel is an arbitrary affair.

The lavishness and flair of what especially women wear is a revelation to first-time visitors

Circumcision To begin with what is taken off rather than put on, every Gambian boy is circumcised: in traditional tribal rituals as described in *Roots*, after lessons from a slave in manhood, morals, bushcraft and filial duty with a *kafo/lell* of contemporaries, or more often nowadays by unceremonious surgery at the local clinic. Boys coming up for 'initiation' can still be seen trekking in to the *dansukunda*, summoned by the *baringo* drum. They are fêted with gunfire and a slaughtered goat, griots' chanting and dancing at the bantaba on the actual day. They skulk in the bush for a month or two thereafter, a stick in their hand, their head in a cloth and dressed in white calico dyed from the *woloo*-tree. And finally return home, healed, with firewood and grass to reroof their neighbours' houses.

When girls undergo similar bush-surgery, feminists call it 'genital mutilation'. For most Fula, Jola, Mandinka and Serahuli girls, 'mutilation' is as accepted and normal as it is for

boys throughout Islam, Judaism and much of Christendom. Mothers and aunts, not the menfolk, uphold the practice. And often ferociously so: a British mission doctor in a village up river reports the recent stoning of a government official lecturing on the undesirability (and illegality) of female circumcision. Prompted by the missions and foreign aid agencies, the authorities make sporadic efforts to discourage the practice. But Gambians of every persuasion were recently shocked to see it shown, graphically, on family TV and officially the custom is now condoned again.

For this is *Sutura*, a topic so taboo that even girls rarely discuss it amongst themselves. With prying English authors naturally less. Doctors and gynæcologists, despite rather better access, are not agreed on the procedure. 'Scar tissue confuses the issue', said one. My hope proved vain that nothing more was involved than the cosmetic labial straightening that is commonplace in eastern Africa. Most

Fulas at least practise full cruel clitoridectomy, on girls as young as seven. Glimpsing village processions of pubescent candidates, their faces whitened and their dresses blue, is the closest most visitors come to evidence. Once circumcised, Fulas, Jolas and Mandinkas wear around the waist the titillating *jiljali*s that Aku and Wolof women wear willy nilly.

Besides circumcision, Muslim men share with their co-religionists everywhere the graceful and airy haftan, a practical, long-sleeved, ankle-length 'night-shirt'. Also known as *s(h)abado*, *jalabe* or *fataro*, the Wolof *haftan* is a mispronounced kaftan. Full-dress accessories are the usually matching hat that Mandinkas call *nafo* and Wolofs *kopoti*, and the heelless slippers that both name *marakisu/marakiss* (cf Marrakech). When the haftan/kaftan stops short on the calf, Gambians use its Arabic name of *abbaya*. Popular also amongst Muslim worthies is the Wolofs' three-piece suit *nyete abdu*. The sirwal-style trousers are *tubay* or *chaya*, and *dendiko* is Mandinka for any shirt or top. The *waramba* is often encountered: Wolof for 'very large', it is a male or female garment that, holed for the head, hangs loose from the shoulders.

Most Christians and young men about town are 20th-century standard. (Often their only distinctive accessories are 'tea-cosies': coloured woolly hats either knitted by Ma or bought from a stall in Albert Market which sells nothing but coloured woolly hats.) Compared with their women-folk, the men in T-shirts and jeans are sartorial non-starters. For the ladies of the capital in particular exhibit a grace and taste to which words cannot do justice. The

Older Muslim men wear the red or white *nafo/kopoti* (above)
Younger men about town prefer coloured woolly 'tea-cosies' or,
increasingly nowadays, baseball caps

Señoras and Wolofs from Senegal made a dazzling impact on 19th-century settlers. The rows of boys treadling sewing-machines in townships without a hospital or bar still say much for the demands of women's wardrobes. What amazes most is that so much feminine splendour should emerge from such humble shacks and shanties. Young women in particular now add a touch of (sometimes stumbling) stateliness with their fondness for fashionable 'platforms'.

Women also wear the waramba (above), especially up country where hard-working wives appreciate its cheap and sleeveless looseness. But most characteristic of *la Sénégambienne* is the *granbuba*. Its Mandinka alias of *buluba* – 'big sleeve' – is descriptive. Big in every respect, it drops full-length from a neck in no way décolleté, with seams down either side beneath elongated sleeve-holes. Visitors may or may not need to know that beneath the granbuba

At the 'Ids especially, women's dressmakers treadle day and night
Lengths of tie-dye and dressed dolls sold on the beach
In a *marinière*, atop the Arch 22 (below)

75

two metres of cloth may be wrapped into an underskirt like the lower half of a sari. This *pagne*, *sirr* or *malane* often covers a short slip or two, the *betcho*, and the latter the panties. All this is designed to enhance the African attraction that specialists call steatopyga.

Shapelier ladies prefer the *dagit/daget(o)*. Wolof for 'short', this three-quarter-length top is essentially tighter than the granbuba, with a closely fitted waist. Looser, shorter and popular, the *marinière* is likewise worn with a long matching skirt called *sepa* (a mispronounced *jupe*?). All may be topped by a matching head-dress. And are modelled by the dolls sold on the beach. About the house viz. compound, town and country women wrap a *pagne* around the waist in sarong or khanga-fashion, with or without blouse and bra.

out by the hair-pieces sold on Banjul pavements, decked out in coins, seeds, beads and knick-knacks of plastic or bone, Gambian girls construct coiffures that are often tonsorial feats.

Called in Wolof *mussor*, in Mandinka *tiko*, the head-dress is often a work of art. (Or more prosaically, to quote Mungo Park, 'a bandage . . . wrapped many times round, immediately over the forehead'.) Styling and tying are at discretion: ribbons may be added, gold thread entwined and shells inserted. Solid gold earrings, in distinctive half-moon, wheel-rim shapes, are the family savings worn by Serahuli women. The head-dress is in places a cosmetic necessity: where washing water is precious and fetched from afar, women crop their hair short or shave it hygienically off.

The ladies' hair-styles, like their attire, is just as predictable as feminine taste. Whilst 'pure' Fula women have long unnegroid hair, those in Banjul with similar inclinations must resort to *défriseurs*. The supermarkets do good business with their various brands of 'Hair Straightener for Natural Frizzy Hair'. It would in this connection be unkind to point out that Mungo Park's paragraph on local hair-dos leads straight on into thatching. It would also be wrongly unflattering to add that, boating through the mangrove swamps with certain styles in mind, you might find the pattern of the air-roots *déjà vu*. But these and many other striking styles – *berti*, *jerreh* and *dundubale/duni-bally*, *armandija* and *pess-sa-gorro* – are African delights. Helped

Muslim men are typical in limp white skull-caps or embroidered 'pot-hats'; older worthies dignified by the red fez, imported complete with black tassel, and Fulas recognizable by their conical 'Chinese' straw hats sometimes patterned with coloured sticky tape.

Cross-cultural Shock, Names and Language

There are few familiar pegs to hang associations on here; little is déjà vu

Americans attending our Beirut school of Arabic were armed by their government with a paper on cross-cultural shock. This American invention, we discovered, was considered a risk not of first encounters with Arabs but with us, their British class-mates. By that token, The Gambia's cultural impact should cause not shock but trauma. Being off the beaten tourist track, beyond the scope of school geography and history, the only English-speaking country between the Channel Islands and the Gulf of Guinea has much that is 'exotic', beyond our ken.

With a slight shift of mental stance, looking analytically and not full frontal, you may feel less intellectually lost. Names are a case in point. Your driver's, guide's or waiter's, those over shops and in print seem unheard-of mumbo jumbo. Yet Arabic names like Mohammed or Abdullah are now commonplace in Europe. These the Senegambians have simply Africanized. Having the same problem as ourselves with the Arabic *h* of Mohammed, they have turned the name of the Prophet into Mamudu or Momodou. The same awkward *h* in the Arabic Fathi explains the many Gambians called Fatty (no joke). Abdullah should start with the impossible Arabic *'ain*, so Abdelahi, Abdoulie or Abdu/Abdou is the Senegambian solution. Issa (the Arabic Jesus) and Othman (whence Ottoman) share this initial problem of an unpronounceable *'ain*, so are simplified respectively into Issatou and Ousman. The *kh* of the Arabs' Khalifa is another built-in impediment to speech, which Gambians circumvent with their Kelefa. Abu Bakr ends up here as Baboucarr/Babukar (what Wolofs also call kingfishers!). Amongst Muslim girls the Arabic Zainab becomes the thicker-lipped Sainabou – Sy for short – while the Prophet's daughter Fatima takes on the deeper drum-note of Fatuma, Fatu or Faa, and often the rhythmic suffix Fatumata.

The *Mseu* that men are sometimes addressed by is not the *Mzee* of East Africa but *Monsieur*, imported from French-speaking Senegal and somewhat damaged in transit. A 'yard mastah' is the family head (of a compound). 'Mastah', 'massah' or 'boss' is what fellow men, Sir, call you. The children also call you, loudly and collectively, *tubab*. The Gambians' kindliness is an assurance that no offence is meant. The meaning is in fact not so much 'Westerner' or 'White (person)' as VIP or 'big shot'. *Tubab* is what poor blacks may call better-off neighbours.

Having wrapped your mind round your Gambian friends' names, you then find they gleefully discard and/or distort them. Nicknames and aliases are an accepted idiosyncrasy that must frustrate the CID. In the newspapers for example: 'Alhaji M.B. Njie Manager of British Petroleum … and commonly known as N'jie Dodou or N'jie B.P. has been appointed …'. Dodou along with Modu, Modi and the unlikely Lamin(e)(*Al-Amin*, one of the godhead's 99 'attributes') is short for Mohammed.

Even the terms you recognize from English may be *faux amis*, familiar but misleading. The Wolofs' *Mam*, the Mandinkas' *Mama* is obviously Mother, *Pa* naturally Father, like the un-English but more logical *Fa*. These parental abbreviations, though, are also applied to aunts and grandmothers, uncles and grandfathers respectively. And, respectfully, to you. Genealogists struggling with family-trees (*lasilos*) face problems that Berkeley Rice conveys in jocular patois: 'Karamo Fatty not Souri's propah fadda. He be small fadda. Souri's real fadda be old pa. This be his brudda'. Translated, this means that Karamo and Souri are stepbrothers. Precision in speech or spelling, nice delimitations of family or personal relations you should not expect of The Gambia's man in the street.

Vacation travel is also less confusing if you come to grips with place-names. Many are translated as they occur in the itineraries, but with these general rules in mind you can work out others for yourself. *Ba/bah* is 'big', *nding* 'little' and *tenda* the Mandinka word for wharf. *Tendaba* thus makes a good class-one example before progressing to Banjulunding. Little Banjul – *Banjul Nding* – emerges if you overlook the odd redundant vowel and split the syllables African-style, by consonant groups not in familiar English patterns.

Kunda is *chez* ('the place of') with the founder or namesake preceding. Serekunda is thus 'Sere's place', *Tubabkunda*

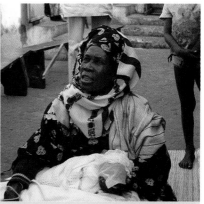

In a ceremony beside which christenings pale, eight-day-old Gambians are named. Family, friends and neighbours foregather with small gifts. Wetting a blade from a symbolic pot (containing water, soap, cotton, maize and kola), the officiating elder cuts a lock from the infant's head and says a silent prayer. Next he whispers into its ear the name its parents have chosen, then the same to the griot who proclaims it. The tuft of hair is later buried; mother, only eight days delivered, may not attend and, leaving kola-nuts and coke for his guests, father may also be hard to find, by the alms-begging griots above all. You need go no further than page 2 of *Roots* for a less cynical-realistic, more romanticized description of the Gambians' famed naming ceremony.

Alex Haley however, when not fabricating facts, based his text on Mandinka village life. With Wolof families around Banjul the ceremony nowadays, while respecting the basic ritual, is also an occasion for best dresses, fizzy drinks and sticky cakes, followed by dancing to not a kora-player but a ghetto-blaster.

or *Morykunda*, where the foreigners or marabouts live, and the north-bank Kinteh Kunda a more likely scenario for Alex Haley's story. Synonyms of *kunda* are *sare/suarra* and the lairdly *kerr, keur* or *karr*. Darsilami/Dasilami is the well-known Dar as-Salaam (Home of Peace) and Madina or Medina simply Arabic for Town. Senegambian place-names, though, are as a subject of research almost virgin. A Wolof in Fula country understands no more than you. The fact that the same name may recur throughout the country at least reduces the problem somewhat.

If in the holiday habit of learning the local language, be warned by Weil's *Linguistic Map of the Gambia*. And the official Radio Gambia which broadcasts its daily news bulletins in five different tongues. Those of the Fulas, Jolas and Serahulis are likely to be encountered less, and the lack of academic publications on them relieves me and the reader of the need to consider them here. It is however significant that the radio station's programmes, like those of Radio Syd, are not only most frequently but also equally in English, Mandinka and Wolof. For although English is the state's official language and will serve you well in hotels and around town, its teaching up river and off the beaten track does not go deep. Even in Banjul Irish priests

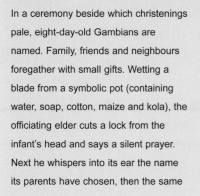

preach to and confess their flock in Wolof, while compulsory crash courses in both this and Mandinka are inflicted on American Peace Corps volunteers.

When listening to local English, proper or pidgin, remember that, just as we cannot cope with the 'click' and other quirks of some local tongues, many Africans display an endearing inability to distinguish between *l* and *r*. Their pronunciation of both is such a liquid nondescript that you may not be able to distinguish it either. Also, as with the Biblical shibboleth, *s* and *sh* are interchanged. The Wartime airbase that was once the Jolas' *Jong Su* or *Joswa* has thus become Jeswang or Jeshwang, and Muslim boys called Sherif introduce themselves as Serif. The Mandinkas' preference of *k* to *g* we know, but *h* in place of *k* is a further complication. Are Messrs Janga, Janha, Janka and Jangka one and the same? This throaty, near-Arabic *k/h*, not a faulty typographer or ear, was why early travellers called the Serahulis Sarakole. All these jelly sounds in a dialectal hotchpot make it impossible for Gambian scholars to adopt the International Phonetic System or even agree on a unified national script. 'Mumbo jumbo', be it said without malice, may derive from the Mandinka *ma-ma-gio-mbo*, a 'magician who makes troubled ancestors' spirits go away'.

Bibliography and History

You will find very little on The Gambia in libraries and bookshops at home (although D. P. Gamble's *General Bibliography of The Gambia* is a thick and tight-typed volume; G. K. Hall, Boston, Massachusetts). Published works on traditional tribal structures are Charlotte Quinn's *Mandingo Kingdoms of the Senegambia* (Longman), Gamble's *The Wolof of Senegambia, together with notes on the Lebu and the Serer* (International African Institute, London, 1957) and Patience Sonko-Godwin's *Ethnic Groups of the Senegambia* (Book Production Unit, Banjul, 1985). The best bird book is Clive Barlow and Tim Wacher's *Birds of The Gambia* (Pica Press 1997, reprinted 1999).

Monolithic booksellers like Dillons-cum-Waterstone's sell guide-books only on The Gambia. A recent article in *The Times Weekend* pinpointed one of their problems: 'They are outdated before they are even published, as it takes on average two years from commissioning to publication. And as the shelf-life of most books is two years, there may be as much as four years between the original research and a tourist's visit'. So, with guide-books *ipso facto*, the more current details they contain, the more mistakes. While none of them receives the annual updating needed, the Directory enclosed with this *Gambia* does, and guide-books are detailed there.

For the rest, The Gambia's documentation is somewhat undistinguished. The *Commonwealth Fact Sheet* is a dated *vade mecum*; expense-account businessmen's accessories such as the Economist's *Quarterly Review* are trenchantly if ephemerally topical. There are period pieces like Richard Jobson's *The Golden Trade* (1623, but republished by E. E. Speight & R. H. Walpole, Teignmouth) and Lang's *Land of The Golden Trade* (reprinted in 1969 by the Negro University Press, New York). Mungo Park's *Travels in the Interior (Districts) of Africa* is a classic of West African exploration, first published in 1799 (and in 1984 handsomely republished by The Folio Society). The end-piece portrait of the frock-coated, top-hatted Henry Fenwick Reeve CMG, MICE, FRGS, FAS, ETC, ETC. typifies his *The Gambia*: a preened and humourless

Batik kora-player

volume, impregnated with Victorian public-school culture but dated also by its odd combination of jingoistic self-righteousness and colonial *mea culpa* (John Murray, 1912). Lady Southorn's *The Gambia* is jollier. Her style and standpoint are those expected of the wife of a colonial governor (Sir Wilfrid Thomas Southorn hangs, slightly peaky-awkward, in the National Museum) but she like many others flounders in the quagmire of Gambian history (George Allen & Unwin, 1952). Two years before the Southorns arrived, Rex Hardinge visited and wrote *Gambia and Beyond* (Blackie, 1934). It is also rather spiffing and pith-helmet but altogether lighter weight, more 'Africa and Me'. A cut above all these and a class apart is *Enter Gambia, The Birth of an Improbable Nation* (Angus & Robertson, 1968). In this the American Berkeley Rice depicts the country on the point of independence with a stylish hilarity that almost stays the course. And with a warmth and affection that Gambians tend to resent. They find that the author makes facile fun and tells home truths too flippantly – but none the less keep a copy in the National Library.

The bulk of most general books is taken up by history. It is not unfair to say that they tell half the story badly. For The Gambia's past, like affairs of state, is 'internal' and 'external'. The former, almost entirely oral, finds little place in European archives. It is the preserve of the elders and the griots, members of a hereditary caste who, accompanied by music (and according to Alex Haley), can narrate for three days without repetition their tribe's generations of families and clans, their kings, warrings, triumphs and catastrophes, their years of abundance and seasons of drought.

These *jalis/gewels/*griots are no doubt important. Attached as 'praise-singers' to each headman and king,

they traditionally preceded him on his travels (declaiming not only to scare off snakes). They continue to be popular on Gambian radio and Senegalese TV. Griots, however, misled Alex Haley to Juffure, and in her study of the Mandinka kingdoms – absolute griot domain – Charlotte Quinn found their 'tales . . . less valuable . . . than the traditions and memories of nonprofessional informants'. Oral historians regard the better griots as we would good historical novelists, and give more credence to village elders and 'tarikas', the Arabic *tarikh* (history) written by the 'Mandink-Moros' of early Muslim families like the Cissays and Tourays.

These are the sources of The Gambia's 'internal' history, which Western records ignore almost entirely. Not featuring in travellers' reports or governmental archives, the historical Gambian kingdom of Kaabu has only just been 'discovered'. 'Only in the last ten-fifteen years', wrote Winifred F. Galloway in 1981, 'have oral traditions become "respectable" in western scholarly circles'. They have been a subject of academic study for scarcely any longer, and the task that faces researchers is awesome. French *universitaires* paved the way in Senegal. In Banjul's Oral History & Antiquities Division, B. K. Sidibe and the American Dr Galloway spent months tape recording the elders and griots. They translated and, by collating, sifted the verbal grain from the chaff, academic detective work which permits the piecemeal reconstruction of the nation's past.

Meanwhile we are left with 'external' history books. It is not surprising that those used in schools tend to bypass

The Gambia entirely. For outside the field of slavery, European doings in West Africa had little impact on the international scene. Here we see the tactics, not the strategy of empire: four centuries of sporadic sorties and settlement, colonial in-fighting with its *ad hoc* campaigns and expeditions. The standard histories are not best-sellers. The doyen (by default) is J. M. Gray with his *History of The Gambia* (Frank Cass, 1966). Having laboured conscientiously in official archives, this former Chief Justice of The Gambia details European relations from 1455 until 1938. You feel, though, that not having to prosecute or pass judgment, Mr Justice Gray has hardly analyzed the evidence. His 500 pages of meticulous minutiæ are presented pell-mell; in the welter of petty events it is difficult to see the historical wood for the trees.

A same-named book by Harry A. Gailey, Jr., being shorter, sins less in this direction (Routledge & Kegan Paul, 1964). It is written however in pseudo-learned Americanese that few Britons find pleasing reading. Its subtitle *An Official Handbook* sums up F. B. Archer's *The Gambia Colony and Protectorate* (Frank Cass). Reprinted in 1967, it was written in 1906, when its lists of enactments, tax returns and personnel, like its far more readable chronological narration of events, stop short. Hughes and Perfect's *Political History of The Gambia 1816-1994* is more recently relevant, and self-explanatory.

Handicrafts

A lower caste, paradoxically, provides the greatest crafts-men. Formed in 1970 and still alive if languishing, the Gambian Gold & Silversmiths Society groups 500 men of the Chem, Jobe, Mbow, Nyang and Touray families. Boys, never girls, are 'apprenticed' to their fathers at the start of adolescence. They begin with six grams of silver for a ring, progress through solid or hollow *argent massif* and graduate to filigree. With the finest rolled gold or silver webbed on a frame like the veins of a leaf, The Gambia's filigree master-pieces are models of the art (though rarer now). A rolling mill and draw-plate with holes of different sizes nowadays facilitate this fineness: older hands used a home crucible to mould their gold and silver which was then hammered and rolled even thinner. Another technique I had not met else-where was the 'rough-cast' use of *coos*: grains of this Guinea corn are set in molten ore, the whole thing fired and the coos tapped out when cold. Bijous encrusted with cow's horn, ebony or (illegal) ivory are more 'ethnic' but equally magnificent.

Silver is imported as stones, not ingots, and gold like-wise from London, Dakar or Ghana but in ever decreasing quantities. Both go into pendants, earrings and brooches; letter-openers and articulated fish; exquisite miniature masks and filigree fishing-boats nine inches high. There are massive silver anklets like Beduin bangles, necklaces knotted in clove-hitches and bracelets tressed like hair. Five-dalasi armbands of copper, brass and iron (engraved on request) are cheap contrasts to silver nuggets dipped in gold.

Wood-carving is the preserve of the Janha, Lobeh, N'Jie, Sarr and Sowe clans, and their work best inspected at the Brikama Market. With the craftsmen often Bambaras or Fulas, many busts portray tribal traits: splendid pieces four feet tall and true to Fula life with three scars on each cheek, three on each temple and two in the centre of the forehead. Technically lax Muslims in this fondness for human forms, they also manufacture scale-model warriors and pipe-smoking hunters, their arrows in a quiver and an animal over their shoulders. These flank stylized silhouettes and two-dimensional faces, but most frequent are the masks which tribal rituals require to conceal them.

African masks are a study in themselves: the styles and significance of the many types are the subject of several books. Some are straightforwardly grotesque, others draped Medusa-like with snakes, or many-faced with smaller countenances beside a 'double-decker'. Small mar-vels from every neighbouring state embellish many hotels; the à la carte restaurant of the Bungalow Beach has a mural gallery of masks boned and beaded, in wood, shell and bronze.

Also carved are drums, combs, paper-knives, pestles and mortars; just-recognizable elephants and 'hear no evil' monkeys; pegmen rowing salad-bowl boats; hippos, croc-odiles and the same antelopes and sucking fawns that,

Silverware for sale in Banjul's Albert Market

Mask at Bungalow Beach (opposite)

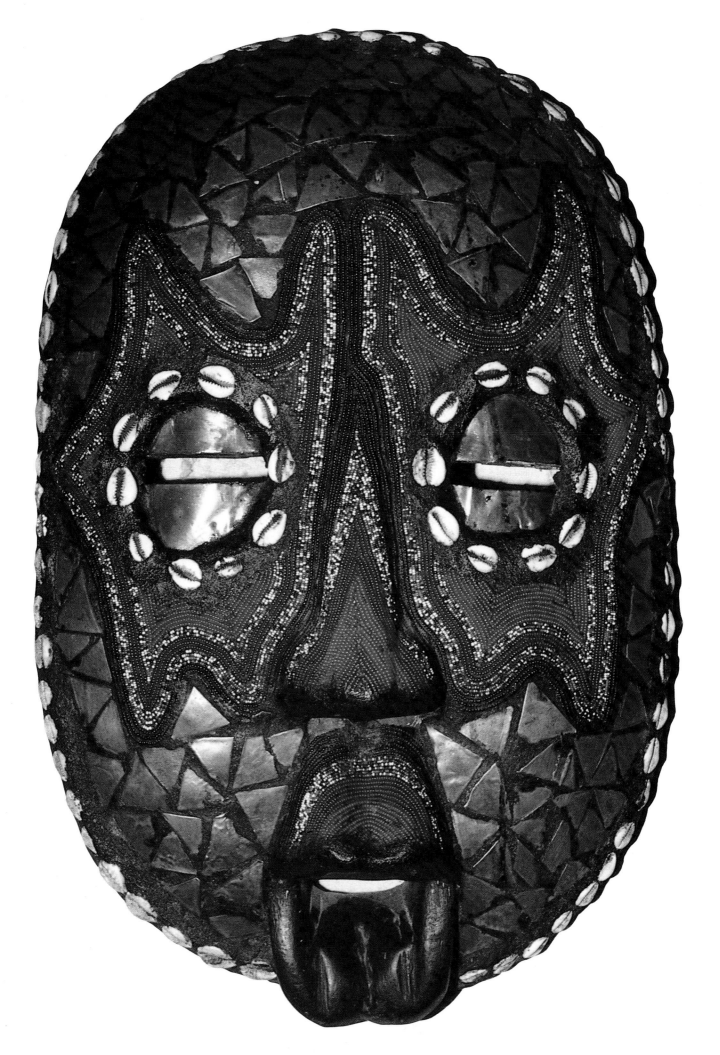

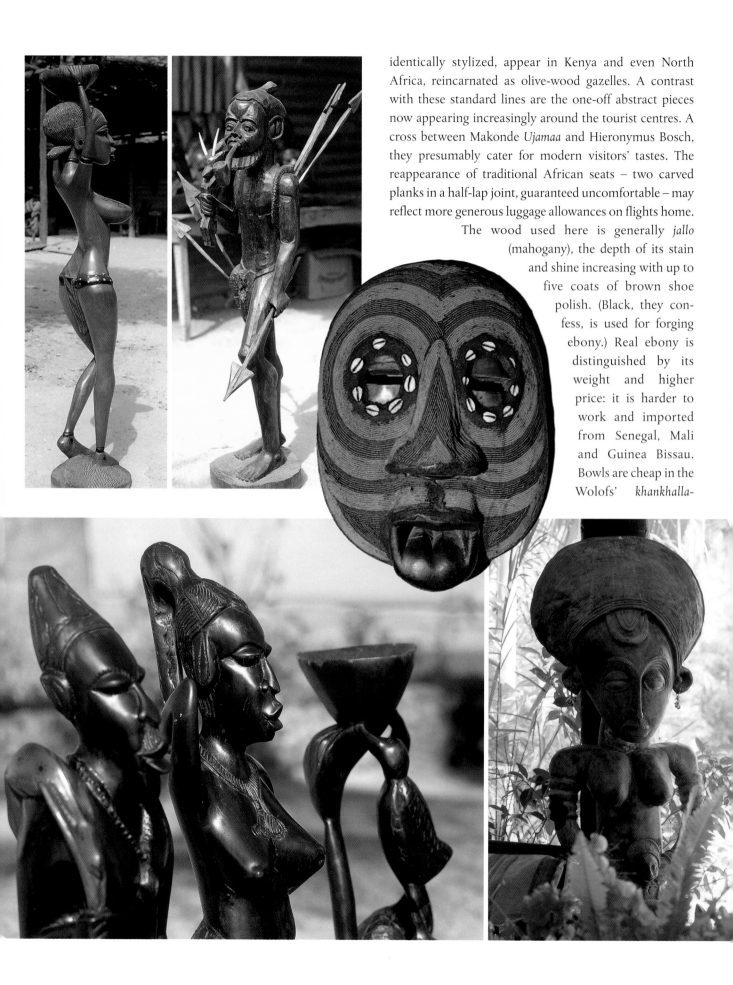

identically stylized, appear in Kenya and even North Africa, reincarnated as olive-wood gazelles. A contrast with these standard lines are the one-off abstract pieces now appearing increasingly around the tourist centres. A cross between Makonde *Ujamaa* and Hieronymus Bosch, they presumably cater for modern visitors' tastes. The reappearance of traditional African seats – two carved planks in a half-lap joint, guaranteed uncomfortable – may reflect more generous luggage allowances on flights home.

The wood used here is generally *jallo* (mahogany), the depth of its stain and shine increasing with up to five coats of brown shoe polish. (Black, they confess, is used for forging ebony.) Real ebony is distinguished by its weight and higher price: it is harder to work and imported from Senegal, Mali and Guinea Bissau. Bowls are cheap in the Wolofs' *khankhalla-*

wood; the soft 'cheese' wood of the *fro-mager*, bombax or silk-cotton tree is used for 'antique' statues, cracked and bleached 'with age'.

Pottery is known to have been made here for the last 6500 years. It is women's work, particularly that of low-caste blacksmiths' wives. Colanders, water containers or coolers; pots for cooking or drinking, for ablutions, medecines or burning incense; vessels for divination or *buntungo*, storing grain . . . the best are made mostly by the Jolas, Serahulis and Mandinkas. Rotund and deep-rimmed pots, two or three feet in diameter, are a speciality of Alohungari. (The most/only photogenic views of Basse show them at the riverbank market Thursday mornings.) Except on Fridays (the Islamic sabbath) the local Serahuli women work kaolin fetched from the paddies. It is sieved, crushed smooth in mortars and moistened for use the next day. Lacking both kilns and the potter's wheel, the women

shape the clay by hand with a bowl as mould, scratch in a chevron or a crescent design (which they later outline with white paint) and fire each piece in a hollow, covered with kindling and wood. The villages near Basse also produce shallow platters, globular bowls and holed coos 'colanders'. In hamlets like Jifarong, laterite pots lie beside the track awaiting transport. Shaped like squat and irregular Mister Men, they have matching half-pot tops.

Nature's counterpart to these man-made shapes (or their inspiration?) are utensils from the calabash/gourd. Its inside rotted by soaking in water, its skin dried wood-hard in the sun, the *Cucurbit* provides several rural receptacles: spoons and ladles from smaller stemmed fruit split in two, and ample half-gourd bowls, often carried on heads and branded in black patterns.

M usic

With captivating rhythm, Senegambian music is Indo-European mellifluous, often prototype jazz

The most spectacular Senegambian shows (apart from the bird life) are musical or muscular: the songs and traditional dances professionally performed by excellent local ensembles, and the weekly wrestling tournaments at Bundung, Serekunda or Lamin.

Fine exponents of 'choreographed ritual', Senegambian dancers are renowned for their dynamism, rhythmic flair and acrobatic finesse. Their forte is the masked or 'social' dance. The latter may represent the Cassankas' palm-wine 'harvest home'; the Balankas' 'warring' to the popular tune *Mama Manneh;* Serahuli women – in a *jembe* dance – working in paddies by moonlight or, with knives thrust symbolically and pelvises suggestively, the Jolas enacting a former forced marriage. The irrepressible Fulas that perform fakir-like in hotels are not the local circus's 'fire-eaters': bundles of flaming grass they pass casually over chest and abdomen, under their chin and down their arms, to swallow them or slowly stamp them out. These *nyamakalas'* 'musical accompaniment' – of half-gourd drum, side-blown *serndu*-flute and awful *riti/nyaanyeru*-fiddle – would be second string to anything, let alone this.

Senegambian instruments are naturally drums and – for melody – koras, balafons and the likes of xalams and bolonbatas. You will see them all in authentic use, displayed in the National Museum and/or reproduced for tourists.

The kora is a characteristically Mandinka instrument. Entitled to 18-24 strings, this African harp-lute has generally 21, in staves of eleven and ten. Its rosewood neck and handles are held straight out, the calabash body on the performer's belly (or, if he is seated, on the ground between his knees). It is played mostly with thumbs. Whilst we beat out rhythms with brushes or sticks, using digital dexterity more for melody, these rôles are in Africa frequently reversed: drumming is a demanding five-finger exercise, while melodymakers like balafons are beaten and musical implements like thumb-pianos speak for themselves. Kora-players compromise, with six or eight fingers resting

The Gambia National Troupe performing, and a kora-player (opposite)

The Jolas' *kumpo* is a startling masked dance. Preceded by a woman whose whisk and water-sprinkler cast protective spells on the circumcised and virtuous, a guide leads in the chanting exorcist. Decked in four sleeved rings of raffia, this kumpo will break the enemy's spell. In a final whirling crescendo of dust he pivots invisibly on a head-pole, his body unseen and the scene unbelievable.

Jola playing the *bugarabu*

idle under the strings, and first fingers at most helping thumbs pluck out a melody. For all that very prettily: the kora has the harp's little-bell tinkle but is less full-bodied, and the Arab qanun's polymorphic nimbleness but is more melodious. The minstrels that play this 'courtly instrument' at many hotel tables complement their 60-piece repertoire with instant lyrics in your honour. (The 'sound-holes' in the resonator-body are for notes: coins clank embarrassingly.)

The bolon or bolonbata is a lesser bent kora, with a maximum five strings tuned to the arpeggio. The neck is curved while its *keno*/rosewood is still green; the body is a smaller gourd, likewise covered tight in cowhide but with the hair left on. It is played only by Mandinkas, Fulas and the odd Guinean Susus (and not made any more tuneful by the large metal rattle round its neck).

The body itself is of rosewood not calabash on the three-, four- or five-stringed lute which Fulas call *hurde*, Mandinkas *kontingo* and Wolofs *halam*, *khalam* or *xalam*. This is the instrument you hear plucked and strummed at Wolof and/or Muslim festivals. (Musicologists consider it a prototype banjo.) Only the Serers, Fulas and Serahulis finger with the left hand and pluck with the right, as we do most stringed instruments – on their *molo* of calabash, cowhide and wood. Except for the horsehair of the *riti*/*nyaanyeru* (the one-stringed fiddle of the Fulas, Wolofs and Serers), all are stringed traditionally with twisted cowhide, gut or antelope-hide, *minau*. Or nowadays more often with nylon fishing-line. You tune by sliding the rawhide loops which attach the strings to the neck.

The balafon or bala is Africa's xylophone (a gift of the devil, Mandinka griots say, to the Kuyateh families in Sunjata's time). Its sound is admittedly not heavenly, more the hollow beauty of Japanese bells. With gourds hung in a frame beneath, its 16-19 keys are struck in resonant and skilful unison. The griots' balafon often accompanies the slightly nasal singing of lady griots, who accompany themselves with a *newo*/*karanyango*, iron bell.

The commonest wind instruments are unfortunately football whistles (which have replaced holed cow's horns). The three-holed transverse *tabiru* and the *serndu* of the Fula *gawulos* ('musicians') are used in tribal ensembles. Or to call cows. Serahulis call *fuleh* the shorter bamboo oboe which they play with four fingers and sometimes cover with leather. The Wolofs are short of wind instruments.

Marking time for dancers, wrestlers or working parties, whistles are blown (and armlet *laala*s rattled) by players of the all-important drums. My favourite is a small drum covered in sheepskin and called *tama* which means Talk. (*Tama nding* – Little tama – is a local brand of bleeper.) You hold it under one arm and squeeze to make it change its tone. The Senegambian drum probably best known in Britain is the *jembe* (which, imported from Senegal, sells as *djembe* in music-shops).

The highest drum in pitch is the Wolofs' *sabar*, which Mandinkas call *sabaro*. The *bellengo* is their big bass drum. Also banged with the right hand, a drumstick in the left, the *kuturiba* and *kuturindingo* are the large and small *kutur*s. They are long, conical and leaned on. The Wolofs sit on the ground to beat the barrel-shaped *gorong* between their knees, while the Jolas' wood-frame of 'kettle-drums' can only be played standing up. Called *bugarabu*, they are sets of four – three differently pitched *tumba*s plus a larger *funyundum*. (Smaller, similar *wimpau*s sent messages to the dead.) The time-honoured beat of the *tabulo/tabala* took news from place to place; nowadays this bowl-shaped drum generally waits for prayers or funerals in each village mosque. Only when new Mandinka kings were crowned was the two-foot *junjung(o)* beaten, *en bandoulière*, with a ten-inch stick. At the other extreme is the Jolas' and Manjagos' *bombolo*, a skinless 'ideophone' from simply a split log. Fill the same with jujus and the boom of this *kumba demba* would keep Mandinka villages safe from war or fire. The Wolofs' *kheen*, the Mandinkas' *daaba* would announce kings or send special news. (Bulletins were limited to an hour or so because thereafter, like the kora's strings, the drum-skin lost its tone. Numbers performed during European tournées may last only fifteen minutes: in the colder climate skins and strings sag faster.)

Like their instrumentalists, Gambian singers harmonize simply but most effectively. Even schoolchildren sing charmingly and most melodiously: in full-throated unison, on key and in contrast to the wavering diffidence of a same-aged class at home. Senegalese cassettes and CDs record not only the 'Musical Roots of the Mandingo Tribe' but something of the origin of southern-state Blues. More professionally updated are the splendid Christian choirs: *Baati Linguere* – 'Pure (Virgin Mary) Voice' – is a group of young Catholics first formed in 1976. With consonants not in an English congregation's slithering succession, but crisp, they overpower the organist whom they do not need – they often beat him to the beat – and fill Banjul Cathedral many Sunday mornings with a moving musical experience.

Senegambian string and percussion, xalam, kora and balafon

Wrestling

Called *nyoboro* in Mandinka, *boreh* in Wolof, modern Senegambian wrestling derives from a deep-seated tradition that probably originated in 13th-century Mali: that of the warrior, who was accredited with powers both physical and spiritual and who ranked in the tribal caste-system directly below the ruling families. (Presentday wrestlers, like footballers in Britain, aspire to and often attain similar social status.)

This may explain why, magnificent village he-men, they strut, dance, spar and literally play to an appreciative gallery that packs the breeze-block seats most weekend afternoons at Lamin, Serekunda or Bundung. Water from the second's bucket makes fine bodies slippery and hard to grip; sand on the hands improves the hold; muscles are flexed, loincloths girded and jujus buckled on before each fight. Between the bouts a woolly-hatted retinue blows whistles and bangs drums, Fulas play flutes, Jolas mouth music and the girls chant to cheerleaders in Mandinka villages. A lap of the krinting-fenced compound in a triumphal jog-trot (and a coin collection) follows. Fingers tapped on foreheads or drawn across throats taunt or threaten. Mock biting off of genitals from a thrown opponent is less frequently seen but of deeper Black African significance: only by possessing his predecessor's penis could, for example, a Baganda claim Kampala.

There is nothing of the protracted Western business of arm-, leg- or head-locks, technical throws, faults, falls and points. The first one down loses. Full stop. One wrestler challenges another, sensibly from the same heavy-, middle- or light-weight class and usually from the same tribe, since 'mixed' fixtures are unusual. Scorning a challenge at first may lead in the end to a more ferocious clinch: round the waist, neck or knee but often first of all on the loincloth (the juju-decked *tobeh*, *ngemba* or – if given by virgins to champions

– *dala*). Pulled, twisted, tripped or lifted bodily, one of the wrestlers soon hits the dust. Punching, kicking, biting, flinging sand in eyes or poking them is permitted but not cricket: in traditional village fixtures it will be stopped by the griot or the offending *kafo*'s 'manager', by self-appointed referees elsewhere, while the crowd boos disapproval.

Banjul and Beyond

Banjul

The Gambia's capital still appears often as 'Banjul formerly Bathurst'. To be precise, 'and formerly Banjul or Banjole' should be added, since the island leased by Britain in 1816 was already known as *Banjulu* to its shifting population of foragers, criminals and runaway slaves. Explanations of the name are at variance. The Portuguese who misquoted Kambi Manneh 'found the islanders cutting raffia-palm: "What is this?" they asked. They were told *banjulu* . . . and wrote it down'. This, the griot Fabala Kanuteh's account, differs from everyone else's: that Banjul means Bamboo, once found here in profusion and first cut by one Madiba from Bakau, who consequently acquired the nickname Madiba Banjol. (The local Mandinkas circumvent the problem with their *Kunu-su-joyo*, Bird's nest Island.) In 1973 the authorities dropped the name which, like that of the town in New South Wales, had honoured Henry, 3rd Earl of Bathurst, Colonial Secretary from 1812 to 1828 and son of 'the weakest though one of the worthiest who ever sat on the woolsack'.

Though birds are still abundant, bamboos and raffia-palms soon made way for an expanding township. Having acquired the site for 100 Spanish dollars (viz. 103 iron bars) per annum, Captain Alexander Grant set his 80 men to clearing the bush and building: with timber from the mainland, rock from Dog Island and mortar from burned oyster-shells. Controlling the river mouth against slavers, attracting merchantmen with its sheltered deep-water berth, Bathurst grew

Batik seller in Banjul's Albert Market

steadily into a loose-knit conurbation. Its hamlets, separated by plots on which 'some sickly vegetation seems to be doing violence to the poverty of the soil', were mostly self-explanatory. The half-caste Portuguese Town; Soldier Town housing the 2nd West Indian Regiment seconded to Grant's Royal African Corps; the better-class 'Jollof'/Melville Town; Jola Town and the Moka/Mocamtown that became

Half Die . . . all flooded indiscriminately at spring tide and during the rains. 'The people catch fish in the middle of the streets . . . and occasionally a crocodile . . . makes its appearance.'

With the Liberated Africans came the first drainage in 1832. A dyke was commenced around Half Die and in 1846 a lock at Malfa Creek; incomplete and insufficient, they were supplemented in 1862 by the

Restored colonial corner-block,
Bedford Place

Gilded kora-player at the Arch 22 (below)

officialdom was quite as much sanitary as military. Barracks built alongside MacCarthy Square grew into the governmental Quadrangle; the hospital commenced in 1853 (and ridiculed by Burton in 1863) was finally improved after 1903 with the help of the Sisters of St Joseph. Around MacCarthy Square and along Marine Parade, building proceeded in 'West African colonial' style: a nondescript (hot and unhealthy) ground floor fronted by imposing double stairways; a smarter upper storey, sometimes projecting and supported by wrought iron, and always surrounded by a colonnaded balcony; walls often whitewashed, and peaked roofs everywhere of corrugated iron. Intrinsically ugly, sheets of the last are worked ingeniously and with unusual style into spires and minarets on richer village mosques, into curving roofs and gabled dormers on Banjul's older buildings.

The latter constitute almost all of its architectural assets. On its low-lying island, the capital keeps a low profile: until the erection of the Arch 22, the Central Bank was the only skyscraper and landmark. Though the Serekunda conurbation is bigger than Banjul, and Fajara far smarter, Britons at least should have a soft spot for a capital planned around a cricket pitch.

sluice gates called Box Bar. An embankment was pushed south from Clifton Road, but only with Bund Road in place did the capital become watertight. A start was made also on the open sewerage system to be flushed by each high tide. In the mid-1950s the whole thing was reversed but, with the outflow still often merely theory, not only the sensitive welcomed the new sewage system funded by the EC in 1984. Since its completion, the 'lattice of open drains' that sullied many visitors' thoughts on Banjul survives only in the *Rough Guide*.

Flooding, the surrounding swamp and motley immigration were the frequent cause of disease. Wesley Church plaques from 1837 result from 'the epidemic, which so awfully raged at that time'. Half Die is a numerical reminder of the cholera of 1869. The control effected by British

The Gambia National Museum merits an early visit: not as cultural preparation for Banjul but as an introduction to Senegambian rites and tribal life-styles which, on a short visit, you would otherwise at most only glimpse. It occupies a pleasant compound of tamarisk and palm: the colony's British Council Centre, which after independence became first the National Library then in 1972 the Oral History & Antiquities Division. Here in 1982 its Monuments & Relics Commission installed the collection begun by B. K. Sidibe and officially inaugurated in 1985 on the twentieth anniversary of The Gambia's independence.

The first objects you encounter have been added since: a beached groundnut cutter and life-size *kankurang*. This is not a dance, as one guide-book says, but a feared pseudo-demon (from whom women, children and the uncircumcised must hide). Masked and covered in baobab-bark, the potent spirit incarnate can still be seen at ceremonies such as circumcision, warding off evil by threatening passers-by and kicking up dust.

Of the three levels inside, well captioned and with welcome ceiling fans, the main hall has exhibits numbered in a semblance of a circuit. The first – I make no comment – is 'Fertility'. Jola and Mandinka 'Symbols of Female Fertility' feature beads and calabashes held by 'women who wish to bear children'. (Barren village wives formed a class apart, called *kanyalang*: for them there are dolls to carry – including an African priapus – and sharpened ritual sticks more fearsome than phallic.)

Second in importance, apparently, are 'Circumcision Rituals'. Despite initiation masks, half-calabashes and colourful 'male circumcision sticks', the display repeats the part-refrain of 'Initiation, Marriage & Female Fertility'. Third is a back wall of handicrafts: basketry and wickerwork made by men and women from raffia, reeds or split bamboo, and weaving, the domain of the all-male *mabo*s. Theirs is the museum's largest display – 'Decorating & Dyeing Cloth' – with cotton carders and indigo beaters, ginning boards, shuttle-boats and spindles. 'Agriculture' is the predictable farm-tools (*inter alia* for planting rice and tapping palms for 'wine'). Leatherwork – tools, dyes, sheaths, scabbards and handbags – is the preserve of artisans whom the Wolofs call *ude* and the Mandinkas *karanke*. 'Products of Smithery' include stirrups, sickles and ceremonial staffs, drills, guns and dinky implements in patterned aluminium.

While smiths, leatherworkers and weavers were low-caste *nyamalolu*, hunters could become kings. They were accredited with magic powers (including *kummaa*, second sight by night) but for all that needed the hunting and fishing jujus which, with guns, slings, traps, harpoons and bows and arrows, are exhibited here. 'Household Utensils' are mortars, pestles, sieves and soap made by baking in the sun a mixture of palm-oil, groundnuts and ash. 'Traditional Kingship' was initiated by the *junjung*, royal drum, and maintained with the help of ceremonial staffs. (The two *chonoo/chorno*s – 200 years old, symbolically male and female and traditionally placed at each side of the royal *bantaba* – have however vanished.)

The *fanals* brought by the Señoras from St Louis evolved from model homes to boats in the hands of Bathurst's shipwrights. The Akus were long known for the Christmas tradition of making and parading these paper-covered boats lit by candles inside. Youth clubs and political parties nowadays undertake these spectacular projects more. (Being for the most part Muslim, they have done so less since Ramadhan came to coincide with Christmas.)

Alongside 'Ornaments' like chest bands, waist bands, anklets, bracelets and earrings, the heads of hair-styles are fun: the *armandija* with up to 1000 hooks; the Mandinkas' *duni-bally* – 'No load on head' (because of cowrie shells plaited in topknots) – and the Wolofs' *pess-sa-gorro*, a cheeky, braided style meaning 'Slap your (mother?) in law'.

Before leaving the main hall, note the holed board-game played since prehistoric times in Africa and Arabia. Most widely known as *bau*, it is called *worro* by Wolofs (and *mancala* by the monthly *Geographical*). Downstairs are drums and many of the pots and musical instruments already described. Plus raffia bee-hives – the Mandinkas' round, the Jolas' square, and all made airtight with cowdung and hung in a flowering tree – and a chamber renovated by an Irish volunteer to promote Alternative Technologies viz. 'scrap art'.

The objects, if not the subjects, are more familiar upstairs: prehistoric tools, weapons and other flint monoliths, stones for slings or hammers, querns and Neolithic pottery. They resemble Neanderthal but, as was admitted, 'it is not possible to tell whether they were made at some later period'. Of unquestioned antiquity, the 'Stone Circles ca. AD 700-1200' receive the attention they merit but are in no way explained. Further displays describe and/or illustrate shell-mounds, earth-tombs and Iron Age village middens (rubbish tips), the 'Ghana Empire ca. AD 400-1076', 'Manding Peoples ca. 1200-1500' and the 'Coming of Islam ca. AD 1000s', with Qoranic texts inscribed on laterite, paper and skin, and misplaced 'iguana', leopard and python skins. One corner is devoted to the 'Soninke-Marabout Wars 1850-1901', another to the 'European Presence ca. 1450-1800' with maps and rates of exchange, Portuguese and Holland beads, and 'Manchester goods' traded for slaves.

'Colonial Gambia 1901-36' is a gallery of administrators, governors and royalty – the Prince of Wales with a Gambian guard of honour in 1925, Queen Elizabeth II on an official visit in 1960. The exhibition is brought almost up to date by 'Independence and Confederation 1965-89', in which the new regime has generously left ex-president Jawara with Harold Wilson and Mao Tse Tung. A final room is frankly educational with plans and pictures on 'Our Natural Resources' contributed by US AID and Peace Corps volunteers.

The Arch 22 came with the new regime, together with gilded statues at roundabouts and roads resurfaced and renamed. (With Bathurst founded one year after Waterloo, many of its streets honoured Wellington's generals. In 1998 most were, like Bakau's, Africanized.) Towering over the roundabout with which modern Banjul starts, the Arch stands astride Independence Drive (which is now blocked off because of it). The cost of its construction in 1994-96 – some £720,000 – was criticized as lavish for so poor a country. Equating it with big-city hallmarks like Big Ben and the Eiffel Tower, the authorities' response may have been tongue-in-cheek but, given Banjul's general lack of grandiosity, the need to mark a new era was a plausible justification.

The massive, hollow-arched pediment on its eight fluted concrete columns was designed by the Senegalese Pierre Kujabi and the Gambian Amadou Samba. Thirty-five metres (114 feet) high, it was built by the joint Gamsen Construction Company and inaugurated in 1996 on the anniversary it commemorates, 22 July.

One lift having succumbed to subsidence in the soft subsoil, the other will help you up to the café and its panoramic terrace. The upper level of the central bridge is occupied by the Arch Museum: displays of textiles including 'Modern Fashions'; agricultural implements and traditional weapons (home-made fire-arms, bamboo bows and arrows, and wooden swords proof against jujus) . . . all 'Treasures from the National Museum' except for the handwritten text of President Jammeh's take-over speech and the stool that he sat upon to make it. A shop sells Arch 22 souvenirs, and upper balconies would offer better vistas were their doors not usually locked. Lining the road below, in a garden that replaced the old Government cemetery, gilded musicians sit cross-legged on toadstool plinths in a style best described as African Alice.

Banjul's new portal, the Arch 22

Albert Market is a tight-packed emporium of local colour (though its claim to be a period piece – and questionable tribute to Queen Victoria's consort – now rests solely on the colonial trading places opposite: 'H. R. Carrol & Co.', 'Farage No 1 Russell Street'). On Russell Street no longer, but Liberation Avenue, the market had its façade reworked in 1983 and its original plaque removed: 'Commenced 1854 Completed May 1855'. The façade as well disappeared in a fire in 1988, and the rebuilding is sufficiently recent for boards to still acknowledge its financing by the UN Development Fund and the Peoples' Republic of China.

Behind the pavement vendors of cigarettes and suitcases, the new façade, arcaded, is two storeys of numbered and roller-shuttered shops. Upstairs tailors work in booths back to back and side by side. In the first entrance alley you run the gauntlet of money-changers; ghetto-blasters on both sides of the second make the cacophony stereophonic. In the main alleys running from here to the river, the goods on sale start familiar if pell mell: cassettes, watches, sunglasses, hair-pieces and home-made soap; powdered milk, peanuts, ginger-root and jeans; T-shirts, flipflops and the latest 'platforms'; shoe polish, locks and keys, Dutch onions, combs and perfumes; Chinese platters of yams, oranges and bananas, open sacks of nuts, seeds or sugar; toothpaste and 'Special Gunpowder' China tea.

There follows a bewilderment of unknown shapes and smells. Bowls of green *fulano* powder are mixed with water to daub on hands and feet; orange resin chunks end up as starch. Incense is burned from obnoxious black balls or a *churayi santang* mixture of seeds, and tea made from bundles of the Wolofs' *mburmbur* leaves. 'Medecines' they brew from dried shoots of *kanifingo* and the fruit of the *sito*, baobab. Leaf-covered sacks contain precious kola-nuts: yellow, pink and bitter, shaped like shelled Brazils, they are chewed as a stimulant, offered to deities and appreciated as a present, peace-offering or tip.

Built around palm-trees that survived the fire, the central hexagon houses both the counters on which village women

hawk their produce (and sleep when it is sold) and the 'tailoring department'. In a vast hive of activity like a 19th-century workhouse, rows of sewing-machines are treadled beside bolts of cloth, buttons, buckles and thread. Off left, the livestock section is cows and goats tethered to old tyres; a small mosque functions near by; local carpenters work close to the river bank. And between these and the central hexagon, three silversmiths soldier on beside the reworked *bengdula*, the tourist market of batik and tie-dye, leatherwork, woodcarvings and other handicrafts.

Beaches near Banjul

Kotu, Kololi, Sanyang and Solifor Point

The Bakau-Fajara promontory constitutes most of Kombo St Mary, the colonists' 'British Kombo' and the locals' *tubab banko*. The 19th-century 'Upper' or 'Foreign Kombo' consisted of the four districts to the south, which were converted to Islam and first united (by Fodi/Kombo Silla) during the Soninki-Marabout Wars.

Bounded to the west by miles of splendid beach, the Kombos give the capital a pleasant rural hinterland, easily accessible and scenically attractive. Even the name, though typically ambiguous, adds to the milk-and-honey image: *Kom bo* ('the hatred is lifted') or, also in Mandinka, 'dew' viz. 'a land so safe that not even dew will fall on you'. Though temporarily contradicted by the marabouts' warring on both Britain and the Kombos' Soninkis, the two terms indicate how the first Mandinkas found a safe and peaceful haven here after their 14-15th-century trek west.

Cape Point received its Portuguese alias *Cabo de Santa Maria* from its 15th-century 'discoverers', and the name of St Mary's overflowed to the nearby island when Britain decided on Bathurst. Captain Grant bought a first site on this breezy Cape St Mary to build a convalescent home for the colony's fever-ridden garrison. And to hang a lantern on a lofty palm as the first of the Gambia's navigational aids. (The British High Commissioner's 19th-century residence is still called nostalgically 'Admiralty House'.) Presentday diplomats and dignitaries have their homes on the cliffs above but Cape Point itself, where sea and river meet, is now monopolized by a German-owned package hotel.

Bakau is the Mandinkas' *Ba kankungo*, Shore or Coast. It is also a long drawn-out clifftop township which, one-sidedly stately with hotels and villas, straggles along Atlantic Road. This runs on into Fajara like a Thatcherite parable, the right prosperous with sought-after houses and gardens, the left a shambles of breeze-block and corrugated iron.

The Katchikali crocodile pool requires, if not a guide, then a fair resistance to unsightliness and smells. Down the narrow Bakau alleys inland from Cape Point the close-packed locals make signposts superfluous. One of the pool's Bojang owners should be at the entrance with his transistor and your ticket. A couple of crocodiles dozing on the banks, cattle egrets on a circle of water lettuce, often there is little else to see.

Associations may be of more interest than appearances. Accredited with supernatural powers, the site was revealed to the Mandinka Bojang family by a ruler's sister called Katchikali. She first tested the worthiness of one Nkooping and his sons Jaali and Tambasi by begging them to help retrieve her child, supposedly lost down a well. For showing willing, they were rewarded with the well itself, where 'any woman washed will, providing she sleeps with no other . . . before the same time next year bear a child'. Jaali and Tambasi in return rewarded Katchikali with the first thing they caught in their nets: two crocodiles, which their mother put into the well. Eight generations of Bojangs ago, these reptiles (and the *pakanju*-water lettuce which soon overgrew the site) were the prelude to the presentday scene.

When the water is too little for the crocodiles to submerge, the women to bathe ritually or the Bojangs to make *naso*-potions, there is no lack of helpers to dig deeper. The first were from Madibakunda, 'Bamboo' Madiba's place; for the re-excavation of 1981 volunteers came from all around, an impressive collective effort. In 1985 a bulldozer was borrowed.

Few tourists have difficulty heeding the warnings: 'Please for safety reasons don't touch any of the crocodiles . . . without the advise of the pool guide'. The cohabitation of 70-odd carnivores so close to Katchikali's compounds you may find surprising. I have a theory that, having always been fed fish, the reptiles here have never developed a taste for humans . . . but keep my distance just in case I have it wrong.

The promontory of Cape Point (above)

The 'Afro-colonial' Department of Agriculture

Bakau beach (below)

Abuko is synonymous here with wildlife conservation and means, for visitors, the Nature Reserve beside the Lamin Stream. In 1916 its source was fenced to form the Abuko Water Catchment Area; the density of its riverine forest increased in consequence and this attracted game. The attention of the locals, too, who holed the fence and poked in their pigs to feed, illegally tapped the protected palms for toddy and, worse, took to poaching. When in 1967 a leopard made these misdemeanours dangerous, one wily Kalilu called on the Wildlife Conservation Officer to shoot it for 'killing domestic pigs'. The latter, Eddie Brewer, was led through a hole in the fence to the scene of the crime, accompanied by his daughter Stella who continues the story: 'I compare that hole . . . with Alice's Looking-Glass, for beyond we discovered an incredible world we had not known existed. With each step, we became more enchanted by what we saw. We were walking from the familiar savannah into the cool, damp atmosphere of a tropical rain forest'. Their immediate desire to preserve this 'glimpse of what The Gambia must once have looked like' was realized in March 1968 when a 'receptive and sympathetic government' agreed to establish the reserve. Its area was extended from 188 to 259 acres in 1978 and enclosed in an eight-foot wire fence with the help of the then World Wildlife Fund. A further barrier to encroaching locals is the 2000 *malina*-softwoods planted since.

Botanists make their way by the numbered trunks of the *50 Trees of Abuko Nature Reserve* usually on sale with your ticket. In the first loose forest of drier Guinea savanna, trunks are caked with mud by tree-ants and treetops decked with their 'nests'. The path soon drops to the main Bambo Pool, pretty with White water-lilies and statuesque with palms. Planks take you across a swampy side-stream and steps past the first hide to the Education Centre, a cool green 'colonial' structure fronted by a defunct fountain and planned in 1970 as the reserve's rest house. This in 1976 made way for a rather more demanding display of ecological documentation. The upstairs 'observation galleries' have earned their laurels, not

because of the occasionally functioning telescope, but as the camera platform for a fight to the death, on the Bambo Pool below, between a python and a crocodile (who won). Here, or on the two other pools dammed in the Lamin Stream, you are most likely to sight Nile crocodiles, Nile monitors and any number of the reserve's 270 bird species.

Tight, eerie jungle follows – gallery forest, evergreen and fed by surface water (as opposed to tropical rain forest which depends on precipitation). Off left (reassurance for the claustrophobic) there are at first snatches of the open bright savanna, but soon you are engulfed by a wondrous lush dark world. Stepping over massive roots, edging round mighty trunks, you hear or glimpse the many monkeys; some, like the squirrels, may scamper over the path, snakes rustle safely away, butterflies and birds flutter in brilliant contrast to the chiaroscuro.

Then a turn in the track and you face a hyæna. It is safely caged, though, in a compound its kin share with vultures. The wardens at the kiosk here are as welcome for their cool drinks as their friendly information. They will show you round the Animal Orphanage. In the largest, 'London Zoo' construction are no longer chimpanzees but Patas monkeys, parrots and parakeets confiscated from illicit traders. When the birds' clipped wing-feathers have regrown and the primates been rehabilitated, they are released. The adjacent enclosure of almost tame bushbuck is shared with irascible Crowned cranes and caged baboons. Alongside, behind wire, are The Gambia's immigrant lions. The first here was Whisky, imported from the Casamance and killed in 1981 by a puff adder bite to the head. In replacement (and in exchange for two hyænas) the Rabat Zoo sent Dyllis, who was due to have a mate. In February 1982, flown and 'donated to the people of The Gambia' by British Caledonian Airways, MacCal arrived from Longleat. And eight days later Dyllis died – of a virus imported by her consort to be? A second mate, Dylise, came in 1984 to provide MacCal with offspring before dying in 1999.

Brikama's rôle in the visitor's Gambia seems doubly disproportionate. Tour firms include it in trips to Abuko, advertising it as a typical up-country township (and The Gambia's third largest). Divisional headquarters and chief town of Kombo Central, it has however little of interest save for the woodcarvers' market. Its history, too, is more remarkable than the presentday place.

Brikama in Bainunka means Women's Town, the governmental quarter established here for the matriarchal locals' former female rulers. Soninki animists, Brikama's Mandinkas stood long and firm against the Muslim marabouts. By 1873 these henchmen of Fodi Kabba's controlled every Foreign Kombo settlement save Brikama and Busumbala. Tomani Bojang, ruler of the former, even offered *in extremis* to cede his lands in return for British protection, but this – with his troops embarked in 1870 and only a 100-man constabulary left – Administrator Callaghan was unable to provide. In mid-1874 Brikama fell to the Muslims, in June 1875 Busumbala also. Chief Bojang and his Soninki subjects sought refuge in British Kombo. Though disarmed, they built a stockade at Lamin, whereupon Fodi Silla sent a threat to 'pursue them to Cape St Mary and destroy them'. The rains saved the colony: they broke and so stopped play. As a diplomatic alternative to certain military defeat, Callaghan's successor, Sir Samuel Rowe, presented Tomani with an ultimatum: on 29 September 1875, rather than evacuate the Kombos, he 'agreed to shave his head, become a marabout, adopt a Muslim name, lay down his arms and destroy his stockade'. With Fodi Silla thus assuaged and the British colony reprieved, the Kombos' two centuries of unbroken Bojang rule came to an end. Fodi Silla's counter-undertaking to let the Soninkis cultivate in peace (and his good-behaviour bonus of £50 per annum) was forgotten by the 1890s. Now however the stronger protectorate was able to take the retaliatory action that led to Fodi Silla's capture, exile and death, and to the reinstatement of a local Bojang chief.

Ghana Town is self-explanatory, but a grandiose name for a fairly minor place. (It has, like Bijilo, been bypassed by the new Kombo coast road being built with Kuwaiti aid.) The hamlet, inland, is little more than a malodorous acre in which sundry fish dry on palm-frond platforms and, dried, are then stacked flat. On the beach, however, is the unexpected sight of thousand upon thousand of superb orange-pink shells smashed and dumped. The living molluscs are fetched in here by the boatload, brought ashore in buckets on the women's heads, piled on the sand and then sorted, shelled and sold. Given what visitors pay for these *cymbium glans*, the locals are discarding a small fortune.

Sanneh-Mentering is Brufut's sacred place, an altogether prettier and more evocative spot. A short walk from Ghana Town (preferably accompanied by the alkalu of Brufut) brings you to the cliff-top clearing with its simple hut and massive baobab. Graffiti are carved in the trunk, by Allied soldiers who were warned of Sanneh's sanctity and 'punished for their impiety'. While those who left their initials 'suffered indescribably all night' (from mosquitos?), the patriot who put 'Scotland for Ever' was killed soon thereafter, self-righteous locals say (war-time safely increasing the odds on such divine retribution).

The stone at the foot of the tree is for alms: a few bututs from tourists, and kola-nuts, cloth or a slave from the pilgrims who come in the hope of a baby or more profitable business. A fertility-bringing wash costs a few dalasis; a week-long vigil in the mud hut, in abstinence until the alkalu returns with a sacrificial sheep, rather more.

I had the luck to arrive once at the same time as a group of young wives from Gunjur. Beautifully dressed, all gold on silk and satin, they came with a biddy carrying her knick-knacks in a halved gourd. They first prayed and placed their coins beside the baobab, then filed down steeply for the ritual washing in seawater – a solemn, impressive procession between the lofty lines of palms.

Woodcarver, Brikama

Offloading the fishing-boats, Ghana Town

Sanneh-Mentering (opposite)

Tanji you often noticed from afar, the stench wafting as far as the smoke from its 'fish-curing site'. Since most of the old sheds were replaced by modern shelters, the approach to the village along the Kombo coast road is rather more savoury, and given interest by a new reserve. Signposted variously as 'Tanje/Tanji-Karinti/Tanji & Bijol Island' Bird Reserve, its 1512 acres encompass the Bijol Islands and the low-forested coastal flats north and south of the Tanji River estuary. Established in 1993, the reserve is supported by the Tanji Birders, a group of UK fundraisers some 200 strong.

The reserve has eclipsed (and the roadwork almost effaced) what little remained of a short-lived ilmenite 'industry'. Along the embankment parallel with the road ran a railway built by the Gambia Minerals Company to transport ore from its mines at Batukunku and Fantatinting to a 'wet mill' near Brufut. Abandoned because of unprofitability, the post-War project survives only in these stretches of line and equipment lying rusting in the bush.

Tanji begins with a pretty lagoon, a bridge and the civilized compound where the Spanish captain of the *Joven Antonio* breeds camels for rides on the beach. The fish-curing sheds are neither sightly nor fragrant. If not averse to smoke or kipper-smells, you can enter and see the procedure – once your eyes have grown accustomed to the gloom. Piles of firewood stand outside the older wooden sheds (which sometimes made it redundant by catching fire themselves).

Fishing by skein-net

Carrying food to the fishermen

Sun-dried fish pell-mell at Ghana Town

Tanji's old fish-curing sheds (opposite)

The beach is liveliest when the fishing-crews come home. Children play, girls gut fish and, beneath the twisted baobabs, the Serers repair their long bright boats and stretch their nets on wooden frames to dry. The self-styled 'sipriters' (shipwrights!) nail the long mahogany planks and caulk them with *tuppa*, a rope-and-cotton

filler. The sides are painted gay with names, dates and/or Arabic imprecations, a crescent moon (the Cross of Islam) or a random geometry of triangles and squares with a face just discernible somewhere.

Driving on blithely past the police post's 'Stop Immigration & Custom' sign, you reach the Tanji/Tanje Village Museum. This was conceived and created in 1995 by a former curator of the National Museum and Juffure's (and author of *Traditional Crafts in The Gambia*): Abdoulie Bayo. It is very much a collector's home-from-home, lovingly assembled with visitors in mind (and, with its owner living in, open every day of

the year). The need for firewood for local fish-curing has for years caused deforestation here (despite the signs 'No tree felling'): Mr Bayo began his one-man counter-attack in 1994, and by '99 was planting 1700 trees per annum. Sixty species are labelled and annotated on his museum's Nature Trail.

A 'Natural History Gallery' of fish and bird prints; nets, horns, dyes and Gambia maps; turtleshells, seashells, snakeskins and a case of bugs may, like the instruments to play and/or buy, be standardly documentary. But the open-air display in the adjoining three acres gives an excellent insight into tribal life-styles, techniques and superstitions. One local tea helps cure head-aches (if poured in your pillow, not drunk); another beverage from *combretum* supposedly saved The Gambia from plague in the 1950s. Village weavers seemed particularly vulnerable: if their *pagne*

of cloth was stolen, they would suffer from pains in the joints; if hung up, it would not sell well or, if approached by a menstruating woman, bring bad luck. Teenagers are traditionally escorted to their cirumcision by the village blacksmith, whose forge is taboo to women (as are eggs to virgins because they make them barren). Village family planning consists of a ban on wives' having sex whilst breast-feeding viz. for two years after giving birth. Bringing shame on the couple if breached, the method is no doubt an even better prophylactic than the much-publicized *Fankanta*, contraception (which Banjul's Imam Fatty has denounced as 'a Western idea and a threat to Islam').

Gunjur is best reached from Brikama, via Kiti and Sifoe on a broad and generally passable laterite 'highway'. South from Tanji, by Tujering and Sanyang, the beaches grow more beautiful as the tracks deteriorate. Stumbling in and out of hamlets as their main street, the 'coast road' finally straightens and widens into Gunjur. A long approach between citrus gardens and low compounds softens the transition from blissful beach to urban bustle. Which the town centre does not lack: bush-buses parked pell mell, two mosques and two markets, police and hand-pumped petrol, a cinema and even a 'travel agent for rural development'. Populous, Gunjur is a relative metropolis.

To clear the site, the locals say, the first settlers had to raze a termite-mound, and *tungo/guru* viz. 'anthill/demolish' became the *Tunjuru* from which *Gunjur* derives. In the second half of the 19th century Gunjur was a marabout base and thus, for British officialdom, a 'hotbed of insurrection'. Fodi Kabba originated here, starting his long inglorious career a lieutenant in Maba's army, and being first mentioned in (British) dispatches by Governor O'Connor in 1855. Fodi Silla was finally routed here, too, in the expeditionary force's successful second attack. If all this is ephemeral and past, marabout religiosity survives in the nearby holy places, which for visitors form the principal interest of this chief town of Kombo South.

Kenye-Kenye Jamango ('Mosque soil') is the most important and easily accessible. Made holy by the sojourn here of one Shaikh Omar Futiu in the late 1830s, it overlooks a magnificent sweep of beach, with (relative) home comforts for the many pilgrims who spend up to a year here: praying in the palm-frond mosque, sleeping in the breeze-block shack, drawing fresh water from cement-rimmed wells and relaxing at the ritual *bantaba*.

You need stamina and a local guide for Tengworo ('Six Palm-trees') where, a half-mile south of Kenye-Kenye, the newly circumcised are washed. Barren women offer bread in the hope of a baby at Nyanitama-Dibindinto, north of Kenye-

Kenye behind the beach – which, under guidance again, is your best means of approach.

Kartung's claim to sacrosanctity is the Folonko crocodile pool. (Its notoriety derives from the track from Gunjur, which I rarely have the heart to use even a hired car on. Lorries loaded with sand for Banjul have pummelled it into deep ruts.)

The pool 'functions' like Katchikali's, is likewise often covered with *pakanju*-water lettuce and has resident reptiles equally unpredictable. But its site is fractionally more dramatic and, being remoter, less frequented. The authorities have enclosed Folonko's enclave with a high wire fence, and in 1980 half encircled the pool itself with a breeze-block wall. Steps down enable 'people to perform the ritual bath, wash their hair and drink a bit of the water. These people are mainly barren women or people with stomach trouble'. On the camp-fire crescent of cement blocks and logs, shady beneath the *kobo*-figs and palms, you can sit and wait for a sight of the white crocodile.

Gunjur beach, late afternoon (above) and at midday with the fishing-boats beached

Kartung crocodiles

Boatyard at Kartung (opposite, upper)

Kenye-Kenye Jamango, a holy place (lower)

The North Bank to Juffure and Niumi

The Banjul-Barra ferry was once again modernized in 1998. In May of that year the Dutch-built *Barra* was inaugurated to supplement and eventually replace the German *Banjul* and *Niumi* commissioned in 1978 and '79. (Custom-built to connect with the then-new terminals, they could not be used elsewhere – and, because of a technical oversight, could on occasions not even be used here. Ferry and terminal were incompatible at certain states of the tide: then all fell back on the old wooden *Barra*, *Bakau* and *Bulok* they theoretically replaced.)

Boarding the Banjul-Barra ferry

Embarking at the Wellington Street/Liberation Avenue terminal, you are piped off by a siren and whistle ensemble – to a half-hour of dolphins plunging their way up river; boys with cinema-usher trays of cigarettes, kola-nuts, hard-boiled eggs, Juicy Fruit chewing-gum and gumdrops called 'Cough'; blind beggars not tapping but intoning, and vendors hawking watches, radios, flipflops and plastic dolls strung like a Playboy lifebelt round their waist.

Barra at first sight is all decrepit relics of the groundnut trade: the broken-down 'evacuation belt' high on its lengthy jetty, beached lighters and the wire-fenced compound of 'bins'. But buses and taxis also clamour for fares on to Dakar; you hear as much French as English in the open-air and the equally busy covered market; Serers build boats on the bank and, a half-mile seaward, Fort Bullen is unmistakable. (The very local hotel is the price you pay for missing the last ferry back to Banjul.)

This odd assemblage is all that remains of the 'kingdom' that featured so prominently in The Gambia's pre-independence history. Christened *Barra* by the Portuguese, Niumi ('the Coast') controlled the lower river: European well-being, first at James Fort and later in Bathurst, depended to a large extent on the (proffered or enforced) goodwill of its rulers.

Fort Bullen The colonial joke that The Gambia's borders were dictated by the range of Britain's gunboats on the river was an evident nonsense already in 1816 when Bathurst was built: its Six Gun Battery and other pieces could not cover even the river mouth and extra fire-power was required on Barra Point against the slavers still trading with Albreda. This the rulers of Niumi had refused, fearing that such guns could be used against their stronghold of Essau. But in 1823 Brunnay/Burungai Sonko came to power; in 1826 HMS *Maidstone* showed the flag together with the *African*, the first steam vessel seen on the river; the governor proposed an annual £100 subsidy and – frightened, enticed and habitually drunk – Burungai agreed to the north bank's 'Ceded Mile' and the fortification of Barra Point. Two cannons were brought across from Bathurst and installed; discharged soldiers and liberated slaves soon settled alongside in the mud-hut Berwick Town. Named after the commander of the intimidating *Maidstone*, Fort Bullen saw action for the first and last time during the so-called Barra War.

Receiving missionaries 'drinking rum from . . . a tea-kettle', chasing the French Resident at Albreda back to Bathurst, Burungai so mistreated British traders in

Fort Bullen and Barra beach

The sacred crocodile pool, Berending

the Ceded Mile that his subsidy was suspended in 1830. The following August a drunken brawl at Barra led, by mistake, to the sounding of the alarm. Soldiers, ships' crews and civilians hurried across from Bathurst and misguidedly marched on Essau. Burungai's Mandinkas, forewarned, forced them back to their boats at Fort Bullen, killing, even decapitating over 30 Britons. Panic rallied the colony's inhabitants; the French moved in from Albreda for protection; 'all, who could carry arms, were drilled and enrolled in a militia; a strong stockade was erected across the island'.

Coming to the rescue from French Gorée, Commandant Louvel of the *Bordelaise* first co-ordinated this defence effort and in September, with men of the West Indian Regiment, sailed for Barra. But despite the traders' formation of the 'River Fencibles' and the despatch by Governor St Germain of more troops from Senegal, the Anglo-French force was still too small. Only on 5 November 1831 – when one British commander had been dismissed, another suffered a nervous breakdown and most of the French been recalled – did Freetown's *Plumper* and *Panchita* arrive with sufficient troops to retake Barra Point. Repeated bombardment and (when the ammunition ran low) hand-to-hand fighting finally induced Burungai to surrender. On 5 January 1832 his subjects 'publicly declared their sorrow for the outrages ... committed in an unjust and cruel war'.

Transit camp in the 1860s for the Muslim refugees from Maba (and its twenty-strong garrison increased to 230 when the marabouts attacked in 1862), Fort Bullen is not on record as having been manned after 1870. Except during World War II, when the 1st Coast Battery took up positions against the (never fulfilled) menace from Vichy-held Senegal. The fort was in the early 1970s proclaimed a national monument.

While these various actions are well documented, no one seems to know when the building was actually completed: 64 paces by 46, circular bastions on each corner and embrasures twelve by 24 on the firing-step of its brick or laterite-block walls. Standardly inscribed with the royal 'GR' and gunmaker William Carron's 'WC°' hallmark, cannons litter the fort. World War II counterparts rust on the beach, their emplacements on the bastions. Fort Bullen is embellished neither by the lighthouse atop another bastion nor its refurbishment in 1996 for the first Roots Homecoming Festival. This brought with it an *ad hoc* rest house and 'modern shower and toilet facilities' so that now, its brochure boasts, Fort Bullen is 'one of The Gambia's big historical tourist attractions'.

Berending Beyond the Serer 'boatyards' and their *jaka* on Barra beach, the road forks round the magnificent

113

baobab of Essau. This rust-red/dust-red hamlet was once the Mandinkas' capital of *Yesseu* and means 'Throw yourself' (into the river?). A new north-bank road financed by the European Development Fund takes you round the Jiffet Bolong and on to Berending. Just before the village a track to the right stumbles down to the crocodile pool. The attraction of the hollow is not so much its namesake *bere n'ding* (small stone) as the riverine greenery of the small pool and the lattice of air-roots that edge it. Someone soon materializes to show the way to the burrows of the tight-palm coppice in which the sacred crocodiles repose. He

Mandinka mother at Berending

should be one of the Sonko family, descendants of Burungai and owners of the area. It was discovered, so they say, by Sumar Bakary and Fodi Brama, Sonko brothers who lie buried where the women now wash. Berending's supernatural properties, and its pilgrims' wash-and-drink rituals, are like Katchikali's and Kartung's, the only difference being that, if anyone in Berending is due to die by night, the crocodiles all cry the day before.

Dog Island, when you sail out from Banjul, is the first perceptible feature as the river narrows. So named because of the barking, dog-faced baboons that

greeted early sailors, it had in 1661 been first baptised Charles Island in honour of the third Stuart monarch. Within a year Major Holmes' soldiers numbered 119 and James Island (then manned by only 29) still took second place in the empire-builders' thinking. Its vulnerability to the mainland at low tide induced Britain to abandon Dog Island in 1666. One year later Duke Jacob of Courland disregarded the danger and established a garrison, whereupon the 'natives made a surprise attack and cut all the Courlanders' throats'. The same fate befell the Frenchmen whom one Captain Ducasse sent ashore to found a trading station in 1678. Eclipsed by James Island, the place served thereafter only as quarry and sanctuary: the British, by the king of Barra's leave, built Bathurst with Dog Island rock and, during the Soninki-Marabout Wars, 200 women and children fled from Maba to be evacuated from here in the Liberated Africans' canoes.

Niumi National Park was gazetted in 1986: nineteen square miles of coastal wetland and mangrove swamp which, rather like the Mara/Serengeti, constitute with the adjacent Salum Delta park in Senegal a single ecological unit. The Masarinko Bolong dissects The Gambia's part of the park and in it survive two rare, endangered species: the African clawless otter and West African manatee. Leopard, Spotted hyæna, kob, oribi, duiker and crocodile are species more easily seen, especially by those with time to spend on the park's Jinack Island.

That an international boundary runs plumb through the last does not bother visitors to the Madiyana Safari Lodge, and seems to go unnoticed by the Serer inhabitants of its four villages, two Gambian, two Senegalese. The visitors arrive either by boat from Banjul (sometimes escorted by Bottle-nosed dolphins, but rarely the Hump-backed variety) or by road on from Barra, then boat: up the Karenti Bolong to the sea and slow over the sandbanks of Buniada Point to the island's seven-mile beach. 'Jinack' is of course the 'Djinakh' of the Survey Department's map and the 'Ginack/Ginak/Gineck/Ginek/Jinak/Jineck/Jinek' you see advertised also.

James Island, in the language of the brochures, is the Sentinel of the Gambia River. Winifred Galloway's monograph on it is subtitled *A Nutshell History*: the history of James Island is in fact that of the whole pre-colonial country in an albeit complex nutshell.

Though the presentday patch of baobabs and crumbling walls gives little indication of its past importance, James Island with Albreda and Juffure constitute The Gambia's most popular river excursion.

After Tristan Nunes (the Portuguese Nuno Tristão) had in 1447 seen the Gambia and died, the Venetian Luiz de Cadamosto was sent south by Portugal's Prince Henry the Navigator (whose mother, most English historians hasten to add, was daughter of 'our John of Gaunt'). Joining forces with Antoniotto Usodimare, Cadamosto entered the river mouth in 1455, but the crews of their three caravels mutinied at the sight of the natives' canoes. They returned in 1456 and, sailing up to Badibu, passed a small island 'shaped like a smoothing iron'. Here they buried a sailor named Andrew, whence the original 'St Andrew's Island'. The two explorers failed in their quest for the riches of Timbuktu and/or the source of the Nile, but they did make friendly contact with the rulers of Badibu and Niumi. Diego Gomez in 1458 continued the search for the kingdom of Prester John, accompanied by an abbot of Soto de Cassa who made the first conversions. But with Philip II of Spain's seizure of the Portuguese throne in 1580, the 'Portingales' in Africa became increasingly detached. Convicts and refugees from the Inquisition, Moors and Jews expelled in 1609, they proved better traders than evangelists and, sowing their seeds with useful ambiguity, left to The Gambia both cash crops from the Americas and the mulatto Señoras.

Dispossessed by Philip II, the Portuguese pretender (one Antonio, prior of Crato) fled from Lisbon to the English court, where he survived by selling the Portuguese crown jewels and 'exclusive trading rights'. In 1588 Elizabeth I confirmed his ten-year grant of the last to a group of London and Devonshire merchants, whereas James I in 1619 preferred 'English gentlemen' for the 'exclusive right of trade to Guinea and Binney' (Benin). These odd early monopolies on speculative trade in unknown parts were often unexpectedly effective. Edward IV had in 1483 prevented two English ships sailing to 'Guinea'. Still in deference to Portuguese rights, Francis I restricted Frenchmen likewise in 1529 and, prior to Antonio's arrival, Elizabeth limited English ships to waters in which the king of Portugal 'hath not presentlie domaine, obedience and tribute'.

The various English 'patentees' did not enjoy such guarantees. The Guinea

Tobago from his godfather, England/Scotland's king James I/VI. And needing slaves for his plantations there, he sent to the king of Niumi for a plot of land at Juffure. With this source of water and firewood on shore, Courlanders under one Major Fock built the first fort on St Andrew's Island in 1651. Another was reportedly constructed on St Mary's Island (likewise leased from the king of Niumi). During The Gambia's Baltic decade, a stalwart commandant called Otto Stiel maintained such relations with the local populace that they helped him see off French and Dutch intruders (speciously entitled to Courland

ensure the safety of his garrison on Dog Island. Having ousted Otto Stiel and his seven remaining men and women, he established Britain's first West African outpost on St Andrew's Island. Which he renamed after James, the then Duke of York and Charles II's future successor.

By 1672 the Royal Adventurers were bankrupt, and replaced by the Royal African Company. The Company of Merchants Trading to Africa took over in 1752, and all maintained on James Island a poorly supplied and sporadic garrison of soldiers, artisans, clerks, gardeners, 'linguister'-interpreters and 'factors' in charge of the trading-post 'factory'.

James Island, fort and jetty

Company is less known for its mercantile success than for *The Golden Trade*, written by one of its ships' supercargoes, Richard Jobson. The subsequent Royal Adventurers, to whom Cromwell and Charles II gave patents, had to contend increasingly with European freebooters. Dutchmen independent since the Spanish War of Succession; Spanish captains redundant from the same and turned privateer; merchant-sailors from Rouen, all traded along the 'Guinea coast' with little respect for exclusive rights.

Germans even appeared on the scene in an odd teutonic interlude. Since 1640 ruler of Courland (the later Baltic states of Latvia/Lithuania), Duke Jacob had received as a christening gift the island of

possessions by the dukedom's metropolitan involvement in such unlikely developments as Sweden's annexation of Poland!).

German-Gambian friendship was cemented even by a visit to the Baltic of Niumi's black ambassadors. Then rudely interrupted by Britain, who in 1661 seized the island in what the Courlanders considered a flagrant breach of international law. The 'Royal Adventurers of England Trading into Africa' justified their acquisition by the pretext that the island was Dutch and thus at the time an enemy possession. Their envoy, Major Robert Holmes (whom Pepys describes as 'a rash, proud coxcombe'), first 'caressed and entertained' the natives of Niumi to

France meanwhile was the scene of similar politico-mercantile, state-run speculation. With Gorée seized in 1677, the Senegalese town of St Louis became the base and the *Compagnie Sénégalaise* the agent of increased French activity along the River Gambia. The ruler of Niumi in 1681 relinquished Albreda to the French (for a monthly rental of four iron bars) and Britain was, during the few periods of peace, obliged to recognise this enclave until it was negotiated out of existence in 1857. A twenty-minute boat ride from James Island, by the on-shore wells which supplied the fort's water, it epitomized The Gambia's live-and-let-live extension of Franco-British rivalry at home. When relations there worsened into war, as in 1689, the British would land and dutifully take Albreda. When in 1695 Monsieur de la Roque sailed from Albreda to James Island to demand a British surrender, he was 'regaled magnificently and the health of each party's respective king was drunk'. The British 'resolved to wait . . . and fight until death': the French fired two shots, the garrison surrendered.

The French destroyed James Fort, confiscated its sparse stores and arms and spiked the guns that their ships could not remove. The Treaty of Ryswick having ended King William's War in 1697, The Gambia reverted to the *status quo*. The Royal African Company rebuilt the fort but in 1698 lost its monopoly of Britain's 'Guinea' trade and thereby the means to maintain it. The scenario is repeated in the Spanish War of Succession, the island's ransom being the only variation. Monsieur de la Roque returned in 1702: James Fort again surrendered. His colleague however, one Captain St Vaudrille, this time offered to spare it if paid £6000. The Royal African Company agreed, but would the French accept delayed payment in three £2000 instalments? The fort, by then derelict, was rebuilt in 1703. Its garrison ('the dregs of London's taverns') mutinied in 1708 but, finding nothing worth plundering, spiked the guns and left. With the Treaty of Utrecht in 1713 the Franco-British situation once again returned to *status quo*.

The Company reconstructed and reoccupied James Fort, to see it seized in 1719 by a Welsh pirate, Howel Davis. 'While he was looting the island's stores, half the fever-ridden fourteen-man garrison decided to join him.' In 1725, on not 5 but 1 November, the powder-house exploded, removing part of the fortifications and eleven of the Europeans. The unedifying sequence of armed Anglo-French bickering, between Albreda and James Island, continued until 1763 when the Seven Years' War ended in the Treaty of Paris and the surrender to Britain of, not only Canada and Florida, but also all of Senegal except Gorée. The governor of the new Crown Colony of Senegambia resided at St Louis but,

because of his 'overmastering aversion to correspondence', his lieutenant-governor on James Island was left do deal as best he could with the felons sent to man the garrison. Too weak to prevent continued French slaving at Albreda, he did just manage in 1768 to hold the island against 500 natives of Niumi who, attacking in twenty canoes, were bent on avenging one of their interpreters who had died unnaturally there.

The province of Senegambia ended with the American War of Independence.

James Fort, ravaged more by time and climate than by 18th-century 18-pounders

Siding with the Thirteen States, the French recaptured Gorée and St Louis, retaking and razing James Fort once again in 1779. Senegal's official return to France by the Treaty of Versailles in 1783, sporadic raids by French privateers, a brief reoccupation by a sergeant's guard after Waterloo, then in 1829 James Island's final abandonment.

The French in 1779 had, with the bastions, blown up the piles which kept the then three-acre island from erosion. Not only its political rôle has gone: its physical area continues to decline as the globe warms and the Gambia's waters rise. For some time yet, though, this will not prevent your taking the outboard to the pontoon and wandering up to the roofless walls. The many generations and calibres of cannon – '1753 24 pr', 'Anno 1777', some repositioned, one off shore underwater – are tokens of the fort's vicissitudes. Its patched and hotchpotch architecture – crude mortared masonry, courses of red brick, some windows' lintels and smooth plaster still intact – results from its repeated reconstruction. Their roots undermining the twenty-foot walls, their bare boughs reaching up to the eleven slits for roof-beams, the baobabs tower as vertical counterparts to the recumbent cannons. Below the silver 'lighthouse' the eagle-eyed find in the sand blue Trade beads and broken green glass from the garrisons' bottled solace: rum.

Albreda *alias* Albadarr (from the Arabic for the full moon?) was the island garrison's on-shore sparring partner during the Franco-British altercations described above. From the first mud hut permitted by the ruler of Niumi's lease of 1681 (and destroyed by fire in 1686) grew a French trading station that was 'destroyed, rebuilt, burned, rebuilt, overrun and rebuilt again'. At one time the French presence consisted of 'two black butlers . . . to hoist their colours every Sunday'; at another, of 'only one Frenchwoman, all the men except her husband being dead' (and she having survived five spouses in three years). Until its resident slavers were ruined by the Act of 1807, Albreda (*pace* Alex Haley) must have been a busy entrepôt. And, according to the authorities, a colonial R&R centre at which 'those who were sick or jaded on James Island could come for recuperation'.

The atmosphere nowadays is more one-hut reminiscent. Weaver birds nest noisily in season by the uprooted tree trunks where the locals sun-dry fish; '*Le Commerce Africain*' is still the sign over one shack-shop. Posing in its frame of baobabs, the derelict, two-storey hulk was not a slave-house, as guides and guide-books say, but the CFAO's 'factory'. The French sold it to the authorities for one symbolic dalasi but it has clearly given up waiting for them to make of it a museum. In lieu of this (since installed at Juffure) the National Council for Arts & Culture has contributed a visitors' map-plan, and the 'Ceded Mile' was in 1995 declared a National Monument Area.

By the kapok-tree on the sandy 'village square' stood the flagstaff that, so the guides say, guaranteed the freedom of any slave that touched it. The Carron eighteen-pounder that recently replaced it, inscribed '*GR*' and made in 1810, is an apter historical feature than the gawdy gilt couple alongside

Juffure, to visitors, is a two-faced place. A fascinating object of fact and fiction, it offers, like a play on a revolving stage, two totally different scenarios. Programmed by *Roots*, most pilgrim-spectators enjoy the evocative if primitive Mandinka-village scene. They dutifully suspend disbelief and wonder at the sight of 'Kunta's bantaba tree', the 'Kinteh Kunda compound' and the widow of griot Fofana who, perched on the ancestral canopied bed and clutching her framed and faded cover-feature magazine, poses as a flesh-and-blood link with our misplaced hero.

But Alex Haley devotees will search in vain for any nearby 'village bolong . . . which took' the Kinte womenfolk 'around a turn into a wider tributary… twisting inland from the Gambia River'. They must also turn a blind eye to the 'Portuguese chapel' and, similarly a stone's throw away, the long-established French outpost at Albreda. These are part of Juffure's other décor, that of historical reality. Three hundred years before Kunta Kinte's time the Portuguese founded the first Juffure, north-east of the present site and named San Domingo. This in local parlance soon became *San Dimonko*, further corrupted into *Sandi Munko Joyo* as the later local alias for James Island. The two-floored 'Portuguese chapel' was probably a shop, store or home. Visible from the track a half-kilometre on from the Albreda-Juffure crossing, it is one of The Gambia's better ruins: small (ten paces square) but unexpectedly tall, with neat courses of mortar between its laterite blocks, patches of plaster still intact and a yellow-brick arch over one lower window.

The Juffure ceded to the Courlanders was probably closer to the present-day site. The Dutchmen captured whilst trying to evict them in 1660; Major Holmes' soldiers disembarking one year later; the African Company's agents that acquired a plot at 'Gilliflee'; the British garrison of the fort erected here in 1721; the French and English 'factors' who, well into Kunta Kinte's time, 'traded side by side in the village' of 'Gilliflee', 'Jithrey' or 'Jillifrey'… none lent credibility to the Haley theory that Juffure – 'four days up-river from the coast' – was the authentic birthplace of his historical Gambian ancestor.

In the early 1980s I realised that *Roots* did not tally with the facts and debunked

it in a *Gambia Holiday Guide* published in 1983. I later learned that a Swedish journalist had come to the same conclusion earlier. His exposé prompted Haley to sue – but then pay out handsomely to have the article suppressed. I had no such luck. Just a tingle of gratification in 1993 when, one year after the author died rich and famous from the fraud, his archives revealed that the Kunta Kinte 'legend' had in fact been bunkum.

None of which detracts from the impact Haley's novel and TV series had in making the horrors of the slave-trade better known. (The Gambians' response has been to shift the emphasis from the American author to a generalized remembrance that they galvanize into an International Roots Homecoming Festival each June.) The history of the iniquitous commerce in 'black ivory' is documented well in the Juffure Museum. To the right of the track from Albreda, it was opened in 1996 in the Maurel Frères' entrepôt built by the British in the late 1840s. Help with the initial display came from as far afield as Ireland and Ghana, the exhibits and information from Gorée, Hull, Maryland, Wisbech and one ex-assistant manager of The Atlantic Hotel. The academic presentation was in 1998 made more graphic-attractive with painted wooden cut-outs of the slavers and their victims: slaves in shackles, plantation ladies with parasols, and a black child on a barrel-head, for auction.

There are a few relics on show – footlocks, necklocks and the double neck-yokes called *coffles*; buttons, beads, sherds, 'Bronze Manillas' (bracelets) and 'Kissi pennies' (iron bars) – but the museum's strength is its posted history. Taken from Hugh Thomas' *The Slave Trade*, the statistics are awesome: 4·65 million Africans deported by the Portuguese, mostly to Brazil; 2·6 million enslaved by the British, 1·6 million by the Spanish and 1·25 million by the French. Two thirds of all slaves traded were female; ten per cent of those caught died during capture or the 'Voyage of no Return' to the Americas.

There is however no 'Eurocentric' condemnation: the exhibition acknowledges that slavery in Africa and Arabia predated the arrival of the likes of

Sir John Hawkins. Senegambian society consisted traditionally of one third slaves. These *jongolu* could be born into servitude, prisoners of war, convicted criminals or debtors. Though universally outlawed since 1888, when Brazil finally accepted abolition, slavery is far from suppressed. In early 2000 *Time* published the distressing number of slaves still

Juffure Museum mural (above)

Roots memorabilia (below)

taken annually in Arabia and eastern Africa. Both there and further west, voluntary and temporary slavery continues: African villagers faced with famine sell themselves, simply to survive, to landowners able to sustain them.

The interest of the south-bank road on from Brikama is initially, as compensation for the pot-holes, a series of minor historical sites and several very worthwhile 'ecological lodges' and camps. The maps on pages 8-9 should help locate them.

Maka Sutu A first, fascinating ecotouristic project is found on the Mandina Bolong (or rather not found without a guide, there being five overland and three creek-approaches). If *Maka* really is Mecca mispronounced, the Mandinkas' *Maka Sutu* should mean Holy Forest. Local reverence may explain the survival of the botanical delight that two Londoners discovered after several years of searching: a pristine expanse of riverine, hardwood and palm-forest, saltflat and mangrove creek. They bought four acres in 1992 whereupon the locals (the spot's sanctity being broken?) took to felling trees. By enlisting the help of the Forestry Department; ecologically converting the villagers around; by planting trees and flowers and building, the two unusual Englishmen had by 1996 developed their 1000-acre 'Maka Sutu culture forest'.

Brefet For another short sortie into the outback follow the main road on past Tumani Tenda ('the first community-owned ecotourist camp in The Gambia') and turn north at Bessi. The alkalu of Brefet will escort you out from the tidy, Jola-Mandinka compounds and down to a beautiful bolong. A copse of ancient baobabs, their massive corpses lying supine on the shore, marks the site of a former 'factory'. Established by the Royal Adventurers in 1664, plundered by the French in 1724, intermittently settled by private British traders and raided by Albreda's slavers as late as 1820, 'Barrowfat' is now a square yard of reddish rock, grey shells embedded in its whitened mortar.

Bintang is reached by a laterite side 'road' signposted at a hamlet called Killing (which official maps euphemize as Killy). Tourist maps still mention Bintang's alias of (I)Gereja. But of this, the Portuguese for Church; of the base built here by Cromwell's patentees in the 1650s; the 'Vintan/Vintang' of the Portuguese mulattos; the factory permitted to the French by the Jola king of Foni in 1717 (and retaken by Britain in 1724); of Mungo Park's 'Vintain' of 1795, the presentday inhabitants know nothing. In the absence

Toniataba, the round house
Hacking a dug-out, Tankular (upper left)
Bwiam, Wolof girl and iron pot

of local guides, one looks for historical spoor: a site near the bolong, any trading station's lifeline; ideally on an eminence, for coolness and ease of defence; perhaps surrounded by baobabs (from seeds placed in Portuguese tombs) . . . and sure enough, left of the jetty, the small hill was strewn with graves and masonry, until they were obliterated by a recent Italian project. Unless an incurable antiquarian, you may think the journey better justified by the Bintang Bolong Lodge, built on stilts above the tidal flats and mangroves.

Bwiam is named after its original owner, one Bwiamu Sambu, and famed (all things being relative) for its enigmatic

commissioners' and six of their Gambian escort. The chieftain responsible was hanged instanter and his village of Dumbutu destroyed. Rebuilt, it now bestrides the junction to the national park headquarters.

The reserve was set up in 1987 at Eddie Brewer's prompting and with funds from US AID but, after both disappeared, its development became spasmodic. Tourism improving and revenue increasing, Kiang West is now back in business as the most accessible and rewarding reserve up river, with a visitors' centre and self-catering accommodation at the Dumbutu headquarters and, more importantly, the greatest range of species and most varied habitats. Forty-four square miles of deciduous and riverine woodland, Guinea savanna, tidal flats and mangrove creeks, it also boasts the Gambian singularity of cliffs all of 70 feet high.

The attractions are not only birds (some 300 recorded species, and 21 birds of prey) and animals (every species resident in The Gambia being represented here). There is history, too, the Warden hastens to point out: in a patch of paving from a Portuguese trading station and vestiges of a *kollon* (well) which, situated near the clifftop viewing shelter, gave its name to this Tubab Kollon Point.

iron pot. It protrudes like the conning-tower of a buried submarine, three stumps (inverted legs?) rising from its bird-limed surface. Mention 'Dogon' to passers-by and they will show you along the track to the T-junction close by the pot. They may also recount its supernatural properties. Some *tubab* (foreigners) once dug all day without working it free. 'And when they returned to dig next day, the soil was back in place around the pot.' (After heavy rain, though, it becomes disprovingly wobbly and could, I suspect, be dislodged by anyone willing to risk offending local feelings.) In time of war the rusting pot is said to turn so that its aperture indicates the quarter of the enemy's attack.

Tankular's baobabs shade the men making bricks and hacking dug-outs with

their hoes. On the muddy beach new boats 'soak', filled with water. Shrimp-traps are slung to dry in the stunted mango and in the lowly waterfront compound (where women sit smoking pipes with babies on their backs) hangs the hamlet's only curiosity: a nondescript ship's bell, dating from 1711 and endowed with the power of ringing itself whenever an enemy or shipwreck threatens. A scrap of compensation for the track from Sankandi is the better-founded information that near by stood a Portuguese trading station.

Kiang West National Park is best visited by road via Dumbutu or Tendaba, after the highway has crossed the Brumen Bridge and swung north past Sankandi. At the last, in 1900, the marabouts shot dead two British 'travelling

Tendaba, or the remoter Kemoto, is the best base for exploring Kiang West. It is served by a signposted laterite 'highway' from Kwinella, a hamlet on the south-bank road now known more for its colourful Thursday-morning market than as the site, in 1863, of the only set battle in the Soninki-Marabout Wars. Attacking with an army of 5000 marabouts, Maba was routed here by the Soninkis, leaving 500 dead. (Relics of British intervention – four unmounted, uninscribed cannon – can still be seen en route for the park beneath Batelling's massive kapok-tree.)

A whimsical signboard to 'Tendaba Airport'; signposts to the national park; a school, fish-market and jetty with lovely river-vistas . . . Tendaba (which means Big Jetty) is little more than its visitors' camp. A Swedish sea-captain developed the two-acre site in 1972, selling out in 1976 to a second Swede long renowned as The

Gambia's only white game warden. An unusual item of décor is a World War I naval mine. 'It just floated up one day. We assume it's been defused.'

Toniataba is the last place of interest to visitors before the south-bank road is crossed by the Trans-Gambia Highway. A well-marked mile north of the road on from Kwinella, Toniataba's village centre is dominated by a remarkable round house. Its owner, Hajji Fudali Fatty, is a fine nonagenarian, white-robed and habitually telling his 'rosary' of beads in strikingly long-fingered hands. He is the last son of Shaikh Othman, a famous Mandinka marabout and alleged purveyor of jujus to Fodi Kabba and Musa Mollo. They would visit him, so the story goes, in this very house: a vast cone of thatch on six-foot walls 60 paces in circumference, supported inside by split bamboos, cement-floored and divided by once-whitewashed mud partitions.

With an interpreter, and shoes removed, you are welcomed in to hear its history: 'When Shaikh Othman *alias* Jimbiti Fatty *alias* Wuli Musa Fatty died, his son Lamin Fatty moved in. He died 120 years old and the next son, Kemu Fatty, inherited. He died at 130 and the house passed to Hajji Fudali' . . . I trusted he would live to at least 140 and was reminded of Dr Galloway's remark that 'Chronology is perhaps the weakest aspect of oral history, which tends to "telescope" lists, while genealogy tends to "expand" it again'. The place-name should at least bear out the Hajji: *Tonia*, Mandinka for Truth, which one pledged oneself to tell beneath its *taba*, kola-tree.

Kataba Fort is seasonally visible close to the north-bank road east of Farafenni. Now fighting off only the undergrowth, its ruined walls and arches survive as a reminder of Britain's colonial confrontations in both Salum and Badibu. After king Kolli had ceded MacCarthy Island, his hostile neighbour Kementeng/Kemintang proved increasingly troublesome. Faced in 1841 with a joint attack by Kementeng, the Fulas and Bambara raiders, the king of Kataba welcomed the British force, signed a treaty of friendship and commerce and gave land for the building of the fort.

Janjangbure was built, a mud-brick township, when king Kolli in 1823 ceded to Britain the island of the same name (which means Refuge). First christened Lemain(e), the island was later renamed in honour of Sir Charles MacCarthy, the African administrator so opposed to slavery that, by pressurizing a reluctant Earl of Bathurst, he succeeded in having Grant sent from Gorée and Bathurst built. Whether the late name of Georgetown commemorated Britain's third Hanoverian, who had recently died after ten years of well-documented 'madness', or his heir George IV, 'an undutiful son, bad husband and callous father, least regretted by those who knew him best', really does not matter.

As headquarters of the Central River (ex-MacCarthy Island) Division, The Gambia's unofficial 'up-country capital' still has much of an old-time trading outpost. The post office might have been an English chapel with its now-disused doorway Gothic-arched. Beside it, the old government rest house has the customary corrugated iron distinguished by unusual whirls and frills. The Home Government of the 1820s may have boggled at permanent building, resting content with the island's mud-brick Fort George and Fort Fatota, but the DC's headquarters is a splendid colonial pile.

From the post office, police post and a new and very narrative memorial, you can walk up the desultory main street (which is even more desultory since the south-bank road was surfaced and the river steamer sank). The long, orange-shuttered frontage of the Methodist Church and primary school seems a disappointing upshot to the years and endeavours that the Wesleyans spent here. Permitted by the king of Kataba to quarry mainland rock after 1827, merchants from Bathurst built the first stores and John Morgan the first mission station. Its congregation was swelled by the Liberated Africans and discharged soldiers settled up river. Its educational mission grew into the famous Chiefs' School reserved for the *seyfolu*'s sons (and rebuilt by the government in 1927). Then renamed the Armitage High School, it remains The Gambia's only secondary boarding establishment.

The roofless hulk of the so-called 'slave market' is unmistakable on the island's north bank. Not only self-appointed guides, even knowledgeable elders point out the wall-rings for the 'shackled and manacled slaves' inside. They are more likely to have served, I think, for bolting the doors or hitching horses. Apart from East Africa's crudely walled pens, physical vestiges of the slave-trade are few. The reason is simple: as a non-perishable commodity, human beings did not need expensive entrepôts. Gables here indicate a once-ridged roof, to keep rain off precious trading goods, not slaves; a slave-pen would not have been, as this is, floored with tiles; the regular arched doorways, neatly rimmed

in brick, and generous windows subsequently blocked are scarcely compatible with a prison.

The problem is compounded, prominently, by new signs near by: 'Attention Attention! . . . Visit the Horrors of Slavery . . . Slaves underground room . . . Tip box available for any offer'. Given the township's obvious poverty, it might have been charitable not to let the truth intrude. That Janjangbure was established by the British in the 1820s is nowhere denied. There is no suggestion of substantial construction prior to 1827, when the first building rock was imported. And Britain abolished slavery in 1807.

Mungo Park Memorial Only those who brave the north-bank ferry and either a hired boat or the track through Karantaba have a chance or making out the plaque on the plain cement obelisk that honours Britain's greatest West African explorer. 'Near this spot Mungo Park set out on the 2nd December 1795 and the 4th May 1805 on his travels to explore the course of the Niger.' The spot was Pisania, a then-prosperous, long-

vanished trading station. In December 1795 the 24-year-old Scottish doctor commenced the lonely and epic trek recounted modestly yet with polished detail by his *Travels in the Interior of Africa*. The second departure in 1805 was again under the auspices of the African Association, but this *Mission to the Interior of Africa* had military and political objectives also. Park was given a commission and an escort of 250 soldiers 'for the purpose of dislodging the French from Albreda . . . of re-establishing English factories in the River Gambia, and of extending the relations of commerce with that and the neighbouring countries'. Frequently at loggerheads with the African Corps' Lieutenant Martyn and encumbered by his retinue (a clumsy contrast to the first journey's black boy, two donkeys and one horse), Park reached the Niger with only Martyn and three half-crazed soldiers still alive. His journal stops short on 16 November 1805 when, near Bussa, all were waylaid and killed.

Janjangbure/Georgetown, the 'slave market'

Ferry at Fatoto

Home by boat with pots bought

at Basse market (opposite)

Basse is headquarters of the Upper River Division and a largely Fula and Serahuli centre. (Its parish church is dedicated to St Cuthbert, a cowherd like many a Fula.) It is also a lively place of trade, made livelier of late, if not lovelier, by increased *trafic* with nearby Senegal, by refugees and, inversely, by Georgetown's decline. There is, seasonally, much local-crop activity. From December to March, tugs may be moored waiting for their lighters to be filled from the groundnut depot. Its eight bins, each for 700 tons, were built in 1974 when the late Gambia Produce Marketing Board took over here from private buyers.

Kapok is collected here too in February and March: lorries loaded with the white floss you see ferried from the north bank in the Dutch-built *Sandugu Bolong*. The ginnery also constructed in 1974 was in 1992 entrusted to GAMCOT, and this joint Franco-Gambian venture has made of cotton Basse's most remunerative product.

Attractions for visitors are the Thursday-morning market (held then because that was when the weekly steamer docked) and Tradition. The market's *pièce de résistance* is its array of earthenware: platters, bowls, colanders and African amphoræ, delivered by donkey-cart from Alohungari and carried away on the ladies' heads. 'Tradition' is the name of an impressive private initiative to encourage (and market) local arts and crafts. With dancers, drummers, Fula fire-eaters and a café/restaurant serving local dishes, its spinners, dyers, weavers, potters and woodworkers occupy the last surviving riverside trading depot. It was built for Maurel Frères in 1906 and leased in 1994 by a Canadian lady-volunteer as base for the splendid enterprise.

All this in Basse Duma Su, *Basse/Bassa* being a mat (on which the town's founder, one General Tiramakang, reportedly first rested). *Duma Su* (Lower Home) is literally the quarter that ventured down to the river's edge in the dry season. The rains used to flood it and then Basse shrank to the *Santu Su* (Upper Home) where it is now concentrated.

Fatoto After 1934 the mail brought up by the Travelling Post Office aboard the weekly steamer was carried on from Basse by a 'travelling postman' who, if he cycled fast enough, reached Fatoto twelve hours later. Modern visitors to Basse need only an hour or two's sortie for this 'roadhead' in The Gambia's eastern reaches. A Mandinka-Fula-Serahuli village, Fatoto in Mandinka means 'spread out', which it is, between the mast-topped hill and the baobabs along the swamp. The market has signs of life; on the dramatic banks where the deep-cleft track ends, women wash, cattle wallow and a tiny ferry shuttles when it must. But in between there are only derelict vestiges of this once-flourishing trading station. Of the six colonnaded premises standing in the 1980s only two brick hulks survive. They were impressively built, but on their walls of brick or mortared stone even the graffiti have eroded away. The crumbling white-tiled or red-brick floors are littered and overgrown; concrete lintels top doorways and windows long removed. With the air of a Western ghost-town, this easternmost administrative centre has now more cows than humans.

The Stone Circles

The Stone Circles are a Senegambian enigma. Though similar, isolated structures are found in the Sahara and as far south as Guinea, the largest known concentration lies scattered north of the Gambia in its mid-river region: clusters of laterite columns, numbering from ten to 24 and many still standing up to nine feet high. Their total, never verified, may reach three figures, but the lack of inscriptions and associated objects has frustrated all attempts to define them historically or ethnographically.

Speculation as to their age ('pre-Islamic viz. 15th-century but post-neolithic'/'as old as 100 years BC') was cut short by recent carbon-14 tests which dated some megaliths to approximately AD 750. Skeletons found in the central graves make them unquestionably burial sites. But these, the only facts we have, themselves pose further problems. The graves are older than the circles; the average height of their negroid incumbents (an impressive 5' 9") suggests a Bantu origin from the south, while all analogous megalithic cultures are found to the north: in Mesopotamia 3000 years BC, in the Egypt of the pyramids, at Stonehenge and Avebury, on Malta and even the Canary Islands as late as the 14th century.

Few accept that a tall black race originated here, evolved the Circles without outside influence and developed the iron implements buried in the graves

and used to shape the stones. The region, apart from a few modern mosques, has no other monuments. What lofty southern immigrants buried their dead here with copper and iron artifacts (the trappings of kingship) and evidence of human sacrifice; later returned to mark the sites with designs derived north of the Sahara and, leaving no clue as to the significance, moved on?

Oral history viz. local tradition has it that the builders were of Egyptian origin. Travelling with an intelligent driver taught me that the comments of visiting specialists can become local lore. The Circles have been the subject of some 30 excavations since the 1880s (all inconclusive). Anglo-Gambian, British, French and Canadian teams have all explored the area with Gambian diggers and guides, and conversational speculation may well be already part of

Stone Circles at Wassu and Lamin Koto

the gospel according to the griots. (Their 'curse' on those who disturb these tombs of the 'ancient gods/giants' was vindicated, or inspired, by the prompt death in 1931 of a certain Captain Doke and two other excavators.)

Apart from the carbon-14 dating and the physical finds, expedition reports contain little more than intelligent topographical guesswork. That relatively few workers could have quickly chiselled even the largest ten-ton columns because freshly quarried laterite is soft (hardening only after exposure to the air). That the iron tools none the less required would have been available locally because laterite contains ore-quality iron (which is known to have been smelted here since circa 500 BC). That taller stones were slid into upright position by means of an encircling trench (because the same stones have fallen back outwards into the trenches' soft refill). What is more challenging and as yet unknown is why designs and sizes vary, with stones from two to nine feet high and from one to four feet in diameter, with circles of ten to 24 stones measuring twelve-twenty feet across; why Ker Bach has a monolithic V-shape, why others are topped by a cup-shaped depression, this fitted in some cases with a neat stone ball. Artistic licence is an unsatisfactory answer: the Circles are so similar over so large an area that they must have been the work of a single society.